I0763256

THERE WAS A PROBLEM WITH SEVERAL OF THE PAGES IN *"MY LIFE IN GERMANY BEFORE AND AFTER JANUARY 30, 1933": A GUIDE TO A MANUSCRIPT COLLECTION AT HOUGHTON LIBRARY, HARVARD UNIVERSITY*. WE APOLOGIZE FOR ANY INCONVENIENCE; ATTACHED ARE THE CORRECTED VERSIONS FOR PAGES:

97
103
107

Australia.

A self-educated writer, the author describes his youth as an apprentice and member of socialist youth groups. The memoir chronicles the author's education in night school and his perceptive observations of everyday life in the 1930s. He leaves Germany in early 1939.

23 pp., typescript.

182. **Reiner, Max**; b: March 23, 1883, Czernovitz/Bukowina [d: 1944, Jerusalem]; Jewish, m; journalist, editor; last German residence: Berlin, 1940: Jerusalem.

A well-known Berlin journalist and editor for Ullstein publishing house, the author begins his lengthy and lively memoir with a description of Berlin and its culture before and after 1914. War and revolution, the inflation, and the Hitler Putsch take up the first half of the manuscript. Later the author turns to the politics of the Weimar Republic and the road to the Nazi seizure of power. Although these events and the developments up to 1936 are described impressionistically, the memoir provides a vivid and detailed history of the period. Much of the memoir is based on the author's diaries.

254 pp., typescript, evaluation; copy in the LBI.

Lit.: Limberg/Rübsaat; Richarz, vol.2; Röder/Strauss; papers: LBI.

183. **Reinheimmer, Dr. Hans**; Catholic, m; physicist; last German residence: Berlin, 1940: Boston/Massachusetts.

This brief account focuses on the author's dismissal from his job as a scientist in a factory after denunciations by a Nazi sympathizer. He also describes his odyssey from England to Argentina and finally to the United States.

13 pp., typescript, in English, evaluation.

7 pp., typescript.

200. Scherzer, Oskar; b: Dec 31, 1920, Elbing/East Prussia; Jewish; college student; last German residence: Elbing, 1940: Bronx/New York.

The memoir, prepared as a book manuscript, weaves the story of the author's life as a high school student with the description of his first love, a non-Jewish fellow student. While he prepares to leave the country, his father is deported to a concentration camp. The vivid description and dialogue give detailed impressions of the everyday life of a teenager and young student.

135 pp., typescript.

201. Schloss, Oscar; b: 1875 Heidelberg; Jewish, m; manufacturer; last German residence: Frankfurt/Main, 1940: New York City.

In this detailed memoir, which was completed before the contest announcement, the author describes his childhood and World War I service in the Austrian army. Otherwise, he spends little time on the circumstances of his life and work as an adult prior to 1933, but focuses on life under Nazi rule. He describes his emigration via Great Britain (where members of his family live) to the U.S.

150 pp., typescript, in English.

202. Schmidt, Gerhard; 37; Jewish, s; [businessman; last German residence: Berlin].

This brief memoir describes the author's university years and his work in the family business, which is increasingly threatened by the Nazis. In the wake of *Kristallnacht* he is arrested and put into a concentration camp. After his dismissal he emigrates to China in the spring of 1939.

19 pp., typescript, evaluation; papers: LBI.

212. Sichel, Hilda Honnet; b: 1888, Pine Bluff/Arkansas; Jewish, m, ch: 2; language teacher (husband: lawyer); last German residence: Frankfurt am Main, 1940: Boston/Massachusetts.

The author, an American, leaves her hometown in Arkansas after high school to study in Vienna and Berlin in 1909. She describes the intellectual and cultural life in the two cities and gives a generally critical and distant view of the German social order. She marries a German lawyer but remains distant from the political developments of the 1920s and 1930s until her husband's career is destroyed and he is arrested and put into a concentration camp. The author describes in some detail her struggle with German and American consular authorities, which eventually leads to freedom and emigration for her and her family.

112 pp., typescript, in English, evaluation.

Lit.: Limberg/Rübsaat.

213. Siemsen, Anna; b: Jan. 18, 1882, Mark/Westfalen [d: Jan. 22, 1952, Hamburg]; Protestant, s; educator, politician; 1940: Chexbres/Switzerland.

The daughter of a minister, the author attends university to study German literature and is an acute observer of the Prussian educational system. She becomes a socialist and joins the USPD in 1919 and the SPD in 1922. Her insights into the politics of education continue as she moves into a career as an educational administrator and university teacher and as a city councilwoman. Because of her political affiliation she loses her professorship in 1932. Since she emigrates in 1933, the memoir deals almost exclusively with the pre-1933 period.

86 pp., typescript.

Lit.: Röder/Strauss, NUC, GV, August Siemsen, *Anna Siemsen, Leben und Werk* (Hamburg and Frankfurt: Europaische Verlagsanstalt, 1951).

214. Silberpfennig, Henda.

Transactions
of the
American Philosophical Society
Held at Philadelphia
For Promoting Useful Knowledge
Volume 91 Part 3

---

# "My Life in Germany Before and After January 30, 1933": A Guide to a Manuscript Collection at Houghton Library, Harvard University

*Harry Liebersohn*
*Dorothee Schneider*

American Philosophical Society
Independence Square • Philadelphia
2001

ISBN:0-87169-913-3
US ISSN:0065-9746

Library of Congress Cataloging-in-Publication Data

Liebersohn, Harry.
"My life in Germany before and after January 30, 1933": a guide to a manuscript collection at Houghton Library, Harvard University / Harry Liebersohn, Dorothee Schneider.
p. cm. – (Transactions of the American Philosophical Society, ISSN 0065-9746 ; v. 91, Pt. 3)
Includes bibliographical references and index.
ISBN 0-87169-913-3 (pbk.)
1. Germany–History 1918-1933 2. Germany–History– 1933-1945–Biography–Bibliography–Catalogs. 3. Jews–Germany–Biography–Bibliography–Catalogs 4. Exiles writings, German–Bibliography–Catalogs. 5. Houghton Library–Catalogs. I. Schneider, Dorothee, 1952- II. Title. III. Series.

Z2240 .L54 2001
[DD243]
016.943'004924–dc21

2001041228

# TABLE OF CONTENTS

# ACKNOWLEDGMENTS

Many years have passed since we first began working with the "My Life in Germany" collection, and any list of the colleagues and friends who have helped along the way is necessarily incomplete. We are grateful to Hartmut Lehmann and Reinhart Koselleck for their advice and practical aid when we first began our work. Michael Berkowitz, Peter Fritzsche, Lionel Gossman, Werner Röder, and Fritz Stern offered valuable criticisms of the manuscript at different stages of its evolution. Our thanks, too, to Uta Gerhardt, Leonidas E. Hill, and Liliane Weisberg for discussing the "My Life in Germany" collection with us. Carole Le Faivre-Rochester, our editor at the American Philosophical Society, brought wisdom and efficiency to the many tasks of preparing the manuscript for publication, and was ably complemented, toward the end, by Susan Babbitt. It gives us special pleasure to acknowledge the contribution of our son Jack, who transformed a drab set of statistics into an elegant pie chart. Of course, we are solely responsible for any remaining errors.

The staffs and libraries of the Institut für Zeitgeschichte in Munich and the Leo Baeck Institute in New York aided our research. From beginning to end, Leslie Morris, Curator of Manuscripts, and the staff of Houghton Library, Harvard University, generously placed the collection at our disposal and encouraged our efforts; we thank Dr. Morris for her approval of our publication of this volume with the American Philosophical Society.

We gratefully acknowledge financial support from the Deutsche Forschungsgemeinschaft for visits to the Houghton collection.

# PART I: EDITORS' INTRODUCTION

The "My Life in Germany" collection of memoirs by refugees from Nazi Germany is a remarkably rich and diverse source of autobiographical information on the Nazi era. Housed at Houghton Library of Harvard University, it consists of 263 files containing the memoirs of approximately 230 people who lived in Germany or Austria during the 1930s.[1] Most of the entries of the "My Life in Germany" collection were written during the nine-month time period between August 1939 and April 1940 in response to an essay contest sponsored by three Harvard professors. The stories of the memoirists encompass an almost bewildering range of human experience. The authors come from Danzig and Berlin, from central Germany and the Southwest, from Munich and from Vienna; they are Jews and Catholics and Protestants, and mixtures of these all-too-neat categories in their origins and marriages; they are peddlers and professors, machinists and lawyers, private housewives and public activists; conservatives and liberals and Communists. Their strongest common bond was their exile, but they had left Germany and Austria under widely differing circumstances.[2]

While a few of the memoirs have been published entire or in part, the collection as a whole makes an unusual contribution to our understanding of the period.[3] It is unified by the vantage point of the years 1939 and 1940, in which almost all the entries were written. The memoirs offer a remarkable panorama of the Nazi regime at the height of its domestic power and prestige, but before Germany's territorial expansion and the organization of

---

1 The exact number of authors could not be determined with certainty. Some files bear the names of evaluators (Devereux, Jahndorf) and contain writings by unnamed authors. Not all memoirs on microfilm could be identified. In one case, nearly identical memoirs and biographies in two files (Hans and Harry Kaufmann) raise doubts about their authenticity.

Names cited in parentheses in the following essay refer to entries in the "My Life in Germany" catalogue. Examples in this introduction are not meant to be exhaustive; rather, they refer readers to memoirs of special quality or historical significance.

2 Not all entries were written by emigrés. There were also several by Americans who had visited Germany or Austria and a few by Germans who were Nazi sympathizers.

3 Other important collections of autobiographical materials from the Nazi period may be found in the Leo Baeck Institute (New York), the Wiener Library (Tel Aviv), the Yad Vashem Institute (Jerusalem), the United States Holocaust Memorial Museum (Washington, D.C.), and the Survivors of the Shoah Visual History Foundation (Los Angeles).

the Final Solution.[4] They contribute to our knowledge of the Nazi era in several ways. The transition from democracy to dictatorship emerges from their pages in finely nuanced detail. Most of the authors had lived through the Weimar Republic, and the guidelines of the prize competition encouraged them to write about the earlier period as well as the Nazi years; their essays often compare the complexity of German society in the Weimar Republic, and their own place as full citizens within it, to its artificial homogeneity after 1933. The "My Life in Germany" memoirists also permit us to measure how far Germany by the late 1930s was already a dictatorship unlike anything from the European past. The "My Life in Germany" authors knew, and struggled to make the Harvard professors aware, that an unprecedented transformation of language, laws, and every other aspect of life was under way. At the same time they offer vivid testimony to the particularity of individual experience: even though they may be categorized by gender, class, occupation, religious background, and region, the authors experience the events of the early and mid-twentieth century from idiosyncratic perspectives. Their stories permit the retrospective reader to appreciate how little generic categories such as "Jewish," "doctor," or "Prussian" (or for that matter "German") may say about the texture of personal experience between 1933 and 1940. No historian can dispense with general social categories. But the collection also preserves the testimony of characters who elude the grand overview: the dentist's wife, the dog breeder, the chess virtuoso, the American married to a Viennese lawyer, the acrobat's daughter. Such individuals were not so much eccentric as exemplary for the bustling diversity of Weimar German society; they, too, have their place in a critical remembrance of the era. Finally, the memoirists record many varieties of self-assertion in the early years of the Third Reich. They maintained their personal dignity and public values through forms of behavior ranging from cautious persistence to spectacular acts of courage. Very few of the authors were purely heroic or purely passive; rather their stories capture the concrete possibilities of response to Nazi rule.

Only limited use has been made of the collection since it was deposited at Houghton Library in 1958. Some memoirs have been published in recent

---

[4] On this transition see Avraham Barkai, *From Boycott to Annihilation : The Economic Struggle of German Jews, 1933-1943* (Hanover, New Hampshire: University Press of New England/Brandeis University Press, 1989); Saul Friedländer, *Nazi Germany and the Jews,* vol.1: *The Years of Persecution, 1933-1939* (New York: HarperCollins, 1997); and Inga Clendinnen, *Reading the Holocaust* (Cambridge and New York: Cambridge University Press, 1999).

years either in their entirety or in excerpted form, but only a few scholars have drawn on the rest.[5] Our catalogue and introduction seek to open up the contents of the collection to a broad readership.

## *Origins of the Collection*

The collection had its origins in an essay contest organized by three Harvard professors, Gordon Allport, Edward Y. Hartshorne, and Sydney B. Fay, on the topic, "My Life in Germany before and after January 30, 1933."[6] The contest was apparently announced and advertised in the German-language exile press and in mainstream American publications in 1939.[7] Prizes of up to $500 were promised to those authors who, in the words of the organizers, submitted "the best unpublished life histories on the theme".[8]

The contest rules specified that the essays, which could be written in German or English, "must be authentic" and should contain "things which actually happened, things people did and said.... The judges are not interested in philosophical reflections about the past, but in a record of personal experience." At the same time the judges also encouraged people who had never written to send entries, adding that "this is not a literary competition." The format and length of the manuscripts was left open, although the recommended length was at least 20,000 words, which encouraged an effort beyond jotting down a few pages of memories. The Harvard organizers also asked entrants to submit basic biographical

---

[5] See the excerpts in the volumes cited below, 32. Memoirs excerpted and reprinted in these collections are cited in the catalogue below. Publication data for memoirs that have been published in their entirety are supplied at the end of their respective entries in the catalogue.

Leonidas E. Hill cites from several "My Life in Germany" manuscripts in "Holocaust und 'Historikerstreit,'" Helmut Donat and Lothar Wieland, eds., *"Auschwitz erst möglich gemacht?" - Überlegungen zur jüngsten konservativen Geschichtsbewältigung* (Bremen: Donat, 1991), 23-37.

[6] Gordon Allport (1897-1967) was a social psychologist whose book, *Personality: A Psychological Interpretation* (New York: Holt, 1937), would become a classic of American psychology; he had studied with Hugo Muensterberg at Harvard and spent a year in Germany during the 1920s. Sydney Fay (1876-1967) was a well-known historian of Prussia. Edward Hartshorne (1912-1946) was a sociologist and the son-in-law of Sydney Fay. His book, *The German Universities and National Socialism* (Cambridge, Mass.: Harvard University Press, 1937) earned him the reputation of an expert on the German educational system.

[7] Correspondence in the files mentions the *Pariser Tageblatt* and *Newsweek.*

[8] The contest design and its announcement bear striking resemblance to an essay contest held by Columbia sociologist Theodore Abel in 1933. Abel collected the life stories of 683 National Socialists for his study, *Why Hitler Came to Power* (1938; Cambridge, Mass. and London, England: Harvard University Press, 1986).

information: age and sex, last German residence, religious affiliation, and "social position" (which most entrants interpreted as occupation and annual income).[9]

Over two hundred fifty men and women (and in a few cases, adolescents) sent their writings to Harvard between August 1939 and the deadline of April 1, 1940. The chance to win one of the cash prizes must have been a strong incentive to participate. The five hundred dollars for the first prize could tide over a refugee for many months in most parts of the world, and even one of the five fifth prizes of twenty dollars may have been more than pocket money. To judge from the correspondence, few of the writers were in comfortable financial circumstances in 1939-1940.

We have only an incomplete record of what happened to the manuscripts after they were submitted to Harvard. The files show that all the entries were acknowledged by a secretary. In most cases there was no further correspondence. Sometimes authors wrote in to ask whether they had won a prize or to request help of some kind. Some correspondents also indicated their desire to publish their memoir as a book and requested the return of their manuscript. The contest organizers in some cases made microfilm copies before sending them back.[10]

The published rules left the purpose of the contest vague. The three Harvard professors stated only that they collected material "for the purely scientific purpose . . . to study the social and psychological effects of National Socialism on German society and the German people." If such general statements give few clues to the investigators' plans for the material, the evaluations of the entries offer glimpses of the planned research. Memoirs that fit the general guidelines set by the committee were evaluated by a researcher (often a graduate student) who filled out a standardized, eighteen-page questionnaire developed for the contest. Only a partial questionnaire is preserved in most files, and even in cases where the entire questionnaire is part of the file, only parts of it are filled out. For the historian the "thumbnail summary" and the "conceptual summary" are particularly useful, for they

[9] Many entries did not fit the format of the competition. Authors submitted memoirs that were cursory, fictional, or philosophical. Some lived in Germany only briefly after 1933. Entrants could omit the biographical information; some chose to do so but retained their names, while others used pseudonyms.

[10] We do not know whether authors were asked for permission to have their manuscripts microfilmed, nor do we know the criteria for selecting a manuscript for microfilming.

provide an overview (usually accurate) of the contents.[11] Beyond this, most of the questions are designed to elicit either psychological or sociological information. The extensive questions on psychological profile correspond to Gordon Allport's interest in personality formation under unusual and stressful circumstances, with attention to such phenomena as: "Evidence of decreased and increased mental activity in respect to 1. Planning, 2. Theorizing, 3. Day-dreaming, 4. Delusions etc." More useful for the historian are the sociological questions, which include such categories as family, occupation and social stratification. There are no explicitly historical categories dealing with such topics as national consciousness or social origins in the questionnaire, although the memoirs contain ample data for such an analysis. Finally, the memoirs received letter grades ("A," "B," "C," etc.), perhaps as an assessment for the prize awards.[12] We have only found an incomplete record of the awards. It does not include a full accounting for the first prize (half of which was awarded to Carl Paeschke) and omits some of the other promised prize awards.[13]

The contest sponsors made little further use of the memoirs. Ten authors were subsequently interviewed about their life histories by a graduate student in psychology, and a personality profile was constructed from the interviews for comparison with the written record. Only one published article by Gordon Allport, J.S. Bruner and E.M. Jandorf, "Personality under Social Catastrophe–Ninety Life-Histories of the Nazi Revolution," explicitly made use of the material.[14] Hartshorne planned to write a parallel sociological study but was unable to complete it before his early death, although he did use some of the material in a pamphlet entitled *German Youth and the Nazi Dream of Victory*.[15] We have not discovered any other published statistical or historical study by the contest organizers that used the

[11] In some cases in which the memoir itself was absent from the file and not available on microfilm, we have been able to use information from the questionnaires for our catalogue entry.

[12] These grades rarely correspond to our assessment of the memoirs' value as historical and literary documents.

[13] File no.178 contains the most complete record.

[14] Published in *Character and Personality*, vol.10, no.1 (Sept. 1941), 1-22.

[15] Published as part of a series, *America at War*, no.12, (New York: Farrar and Rinehart, 1941). By then Hartshorne was working in the Office of War Information in Washington, D.C.

material as primary evidence.[16]

*Between Places: The Refugees' Suspended Identity*

Most memoirists wrote as refugees caught between an old world they had suddenly lost and a new world they had only begun to gain. Unlike "flexible citizens" of the late twentieth century who move willingly and fluently between places, they were involuntarily exiles, refugees in search of a permanent home and a national identity.[17] To be sure, even in this respect the memoir writers embraced a wide range of attitudes, from those still unable to separate from their former lives to happily settled newcomers eager to assimilate. A few of the narratives from the United States and Palestine reveal the emerging personalities of citizens of a new country. Younger men and women, especially if they had achieved some measure of security in their new homes, were inclined to explore and take pride in their new surroundings. But these stories form a distinct minority in the collection. Most writers were struggling to sort out the drastic changes they were going through. The break with Central Europe seemed irrevocable; what would replace it was still unclear. The memoirists existed in a state of suspended identity, still shocked by the loss of their familiar surroundings and struggling to survive in exile.

[16] Hartshorne took Käthe Vordtriede's and several other manuscripts with him to Washington. See the editor's Afterword in Käthe Vordtriede, *"Es gibt Zeiten, in denen man welkt." Mein Leben in Deutschland vor und nach 1933*, ed. Detlef Garz (Lengwil, Switzerland: Libelle, 1999), 248-250. On Hartshorne's work as a denazification officer involved in rebuilding German universities in 1945-46, see James F. Tent, *Mission on the Rhine: Reeducation and Denazification in American-Occupied Germany* (Chicago and London: University of Chicago Press, 1982), 48, 64 and 67; and idem., "Edward Yarnall Hartshorne and the Reopening of the Ruprecht-Karls-Universität in Heidelberg, 1945: His Personal Account," in J. C. Hess, H. Lehmann and V. Sellin with D. Junker and E. Wolgast, *Heidelberg 1945* (Stuttgart: Franz Steiner, 1996), 55-74. Tent does not mention any use by Hartshorne of the "My Life in Germany" manuscripts. Cf. Barry M. Katz, *Foreign Intelligence: Research and Analysis in the Office of Strategic Services, 1942-1945* (Cambridge, Mass. and London, England, 1989), which mentions neither Hartshorne nor the Harvard prize competition.

[17] Cf. Aihwa Ong, *Flexible Citizenship: The Cultural Logics of Transnationality* (Durham and London: Duke University Press, 1999).

COUNTRY OF RESIDENCE OF ESSAY WRITERS IN 1939/1940

| | | |
|---|---|---|
| United States: | 155 | 61.7% |
| (New York City: | 96 | 38.2%) |
| Great Britain | 31 | 12.3% |
| Palestine | 20 | 8.% |
| Switzerland | 13 | 5.2% |
| Shanghai | 6 | |
| France | 5 | |
| Sweden | 5 | |
| Australia | 3 | |
| South America/Carib. | 6 | |
| Other* | 7 | |
| N= 245 | | |

*Belgium, Holland, South Africa (2 each), Japan (1).

Quirks of fate, not choice, usually determined the memoirists' place of refuge, a circumstance heightening their sense of homelessness. The carnival exhibitor who decided to stay on in Brussels after attending a fair there, the public health official who prolonged his stay in the US after a sabbatical, and the socialist who made his way to Paris right after the Nazi seizure of power all had little choice about their new place of residence (Bornstein, Gebhard, Broh). Only occasionally, when refugees had family abroad, was emigration less bewildering. A few writers had the foresight and financial resources to exit early to Great Britain or the United States. The better-organized (and much-documented) academic emigration to the United States and elsewhere plays only a minor role in this collection (Hallgarten, Kahle, Löwith).[18]

The outbreak of World War II made safe places insecure and insecure places dangerous. Writers from France, Belgium, Holland, and Norway, ten in all, later experienced the trials of German invasion unless they were able to leave. Writers in Britain and Australia faced the possibility of internment as enemy aliens (Aust, Herz, Mannes). Refugees living under Japanese rule in Japan or Shanghai could not be certain how long their havens would tolerate them. Many refugees dissatisfied or endangered in their first place of exile tried to gain entry to a more secure haven, usually the United States.

[18] Robert Breusch later taught at Amherst College and Ernst Loewenberg at Brandeis University.

Through their correspondence with the Harvard committee we can follow Siegfried Neumann's odyssey from Shanghai and to Palestine and Ada Burger's from Norway to Ecuador. Others were less lucky. Paul Diels last address was an internment camp in Albi, France, and the upholsterer Julius Glaser sent the Harvard committee a card with his new address in the internment camp of Gurs. The trail of James Broh disappears in Nazi-occupied Paris. Siegfried Blumens and Hans Steinbruechner finally gained the coveted immigrant visa to the United States only to die at sea when their ship was sunk by German submarines in 1940. Hermann Krichtensen boarded the *St.Louis* for Cuba in 1939, but along with hundreds of other refugees was denied admission and sent back to Europe.[19] Amid the chaos and danger of the years 1939-1940 the refugees sense of displacement, not the immigrant's sense of belonging, set the tone for the memoirs.

While the country of refuge had little influence on the memoirists, their nation and region of origin bore heavily on their autobiographies. Practically all of the authors clearly identified themselves as Germans or Austrians. At a time when regional loyalties counted for more than they do in Central Europe today, writers wrote not just as Germans or Austrians, but as members of a specific local milieu. The Jewish memoirists were predominantly an urban group, with a high proportion of Berliners and Viennese. Other important urban centers of German cultural life–Frankfurt, Hamburg, Munich and Cologne–come intensely alive in the memoirs. Not all writers grew up in or wrote from urban areas, however. There are also evocative recollections of life in rural settings by Friedrich Weil, a wine dealer in Southwest Germany, by Edwin Landau, who ran a family business in the West Prussian town of Deutsch-Krone, and by the Protestant minister Kuno Fiedler, who describes his childhood in a community of craftsmen in Brandenburg. The strong regional flavor that permeates many of the narratives is not always the product of a single place; in keeping with the urbanization of Germany in general and German Jewry in particular during the late nineteenth and early twentieth century, many moved from the country to the city, as in Leo Grünebaum's evocation of his childhood in rural Hesse and his later life in Cologne, and Alfred Christian Oppler's recollection of his youth in Alsace-Lorraine and his later life in

[19] On the *St. Louis* incident see David Wyman, *Paper Walls: America and the Refugee Crisis, 1938-1941* (Amherst: University of Massachusetts Press, 1968), 37-39; cf. idem., *The Abandonment of the Jews: America and the Holocaust, 1941-1945* (New York: Pantheon, 1984).

Berlin. Geography did not impose a uniform identity on individuals; rather it shaped and reshaped them as mobile members of a modern society. The memoirs capture both the authors' close ties to particular places and

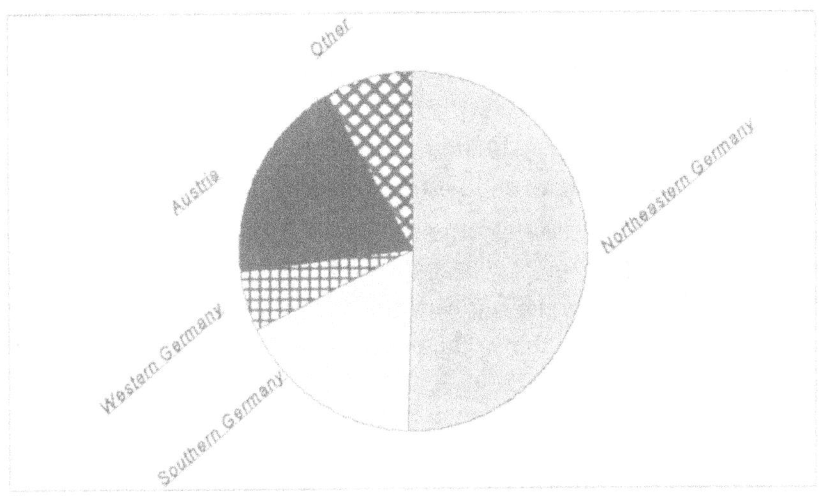


| Last German Home of Entrants | (N= 216) | |
|---|---|---|
| Berlin: | 61 | 28.2% |
| Prussia, Saxony | 25 | 11.5 |
| Hesse, Baden, Württemberg | 22 | 10.2% |
| Bavaria, Franconia | 18 | 8.3% |
| Hamburg | 13 | 6.0% |
| Ruhr, Rhineland | 13 | 6.0 |
| Silesia, Sudetenland | 9 | |
| East Prussia | 6 | |
| Other | 5 | |
| Austria* | 41 | 19.0% |
| (Vienna | 39 | 18.0%) |
| United States** | 13 | 6.0% |

*The former citizens of Austria were classified by the Nazis as residing on "German" territory after the Anschluss in 1938.

**Citizens of the United States, some of whom emigrated from Germany before World War I.

their complex experiences even before the violent disruptions of the 1930s.[20]

### *Jewish Memoirs: Identity and Community before 1933*

At least three-fourths of the "My Life in Germany" memoirs were written by authors who either considered themselves Jewish before 1933, or were labeled Jewish (or part Jewish) thereafter. These memoirs add a wealth of information to the literature on Jewish self-perception and treatment by other Germans, capturing the extreme diversity of the persons grouped together as Jews.[21] They also portray the changing nature of Jewish relations to non-Jews after 1933 with a day-by-day intimacy rarely reflected in official documents and secret reports.[22] Written at the moment of crisis when German-Jewish identity was challenged, but not yet destroyed by the Holocaust, they attest to the close integration of Jews into German society and the distortions necessary to remove them from it.

Beginning with the initial modern discussions of Jewish emancipation in the 1780s, emancipation and antisemitism existed side by side in Central Europe.[23] A political and cultural landscape as diverse as early and mid-

[20] On Jewish integration into German society, see the editor's cogent discussion in Richarz, ed., *Jüdisches Leben in Deutschland Selbstzeugnisse zur sozialgeschichte 1918-1945* (Stuttgart; Deutsche verlagsanstalt, 1982), vol.3, 25-32.

[21] Among the most important recent contributions are Barkai, *From Boycott to Annihilation*, Richarz, *Jüdisches Leben in Deutschland*, vol.3; Wolgang Benz, "Prolog. Der 30. Januar 1933. Die deutschen Juden und der Beginn der nationalsozialistischen Herrschaft," in *Die Juden in Deutschland 1933-1945*, ed. W. Benz (Munich: Beck, 1988), 15-33; Konrad Kwiet and Helmut Eschwege, *Selbstbehauptung und Widerstand. Deutsche Juden im Kampf um Existenz und Menschenwürde 1933-1945* (Hamburg: Christians, 1984). See also Hans Mommsen and Dieter Obst, "Die Reaktion der deutschen Bevölkerung auf die Verfolgung der Juden 1933-1943," in Hans Mommsen and Susanne Willems, eds., *Herrschaftsalltag im Drit-ten Reich: Studien und Texte* (Düsseldorf: Schwann, 1988), 374-426; Ian Kershaw, *Popular Opinion and Political Dissent in the Third Reich: Bavaria 1933-1945* (Oxford: Clarendon, 1983), 224 ff., 267 ff., 377; Robert Gellately, *The Gestapo and German Society: Enforcing Racial Policy, 1933-1945* (Oxford: Clarendon, 1990), 125-126, 210; Sarah Gordon, *Hitler, Germans and the 'Jewish Question'* (Princeton: Princeton University Press, 1984), 169 ff., 300 ff.

[22] Cf. the chronicle of every-day life in Victor Klemperer, *I Will Bear Witness: A Diary of the Nazi years, 1933-1941*, trans. Martin Chalmers (New York: Random House, 1998). See also Elke Fröhlich, *Bayern in der NS-Zeit* ed. Martin Broszat and Elke Fröhlich, vol. 6: *Die Herausforderung des Einzelnen. Geschichten über Widerstand und Verfolgung* (Munich and Vienna: Oldenbourg, 1983), 15-16, on the difficulty of reconstructing individual lives from fragmentary official documents.

[23] Cf. Reinhard Rürup, *Emanzipation und Antisemitismus. Studien zur 'Judenfrage' der bürgerlichen Gesellschaft* (Göttingen: Vandenhoeck und Ruprecht, 1975); and James F.

nineteenth century Germany defies glib generalization. One can point to such factors as religious prejudice, lasting contempt toward a group marginal to the traditional society of orders, and the all-too-gradual tempo of legal enfranchisement. But there were also friendships, marriages, and acceptance of Jews in positions of professional distinction. It is worth keeping in mind, too, that antisemitism was one of a welter of prejudices marring nineteenth-century German society, not least among them Protestant-Catholic antagonisms. A distinctly modern antisemitism began developing after German unification and gathered force in the 1880s, the product of rapid industrialization in Germany and ethnic conflict in Austria, with its mass base in the so-called *Mittelstand* of shopkeepers and artisans, but affirmed by the educated elite. This first wave of political antisemitism declined after the turn of the century. It is easy but misleading today to read the antisemitic violence of 1933-1945 back into the pre-World War I period; it is worth recalling that antisemitism existed in Russia, Austria-Hungary, Britain, and the United States as well as in Germany before 1914. German Jews were not altogether naïve about the mixed reception their non-Jewish neighbors accorded them, but had good reason to regard themselves as a success story.[24]

During the pre-Nazi period covered in the memoirs–from roughly the turn of the century to 1933–German Jews met emancipation and antisemitism with ambiguous responses of acculturation and assimilation, but also formation of a distinctive subculture of voluntary associations; movement from ghetto occupations, but continued high participation in independent businesses, in keeping with their background and with their chances of avoiding antisemitism; and contribution to German high culture, but practice of new forms of Jewish identity such as Reform Judaism and

---

Harris, *The People Speak! Anti-Semitism and Emancipation in Nineteenth-Century Bavaria* (Ann Arbor: University of Michigan, 1994); David Sorkin, *The Transformation of German Jewry, 1780-1840* (New York and Oxford: Oxford University Press, 1987); and Steven M. Lowenstein, *The Berlin Jewish Community: Enlightenment, Family, and Crisis, 1770-1830* (New York and Oxford: Oxford University Press, 1994).

[24] See Michael A. Meyer, ed., *German-Jewish History in Modern Times*, vol. 2: *Emancipation and Acculturation, 1780-1871* (New York: Columbia University Press, 1997); Fritz Stern, *Gold and Iron: Bismarck, Bleichröder, and the Building of the German Empire* (New York: Knopf, 1977); Michael Berkowitz, *Zionist Culture and West European Jewry Before the First World War* (Cambridge and New York: Cambridge University Press, 1993); Jehuda Reinharz, *Fatherland or Promised Land: The Dilemma of the German Jew, 1893-1914* (Ann Arbor: University of Michigan, 1975); Keith H. Picus, *Constructing Modern Identities: Jewish University Students in Germany, 1815-1914* (Detroit: Wayne State University Press, 1999); Mordechai Breuer, *Jüdische Orthodoxie im Deutschen Reich 1871-1918. Sozialgeschichte einer religiösen Minderheit* (Frankfurt am Main: Jüdischer Verlag bei Athenäum, 1986); and Marion A. Kaplan, *The Making of the Jewish Middle Class: Women, Family, and Identity in Imperial Germany* (New York and Oxford: Oxford University Press, 1991).

Zionism as well as a persistent and self-confident Orthodoxy. The "My Life in Germany" memoirs recall a wide range of prewar experiences from lives already marred by antisemitism such as Walter Gottheil's youth in Wilhelmine Prussia to happy childhoods and prosperous careers in a highly integrated setting such as Leopold Dinkel's in Mannheim, located in more tolerant and urbane Baden. Most of the memoirists describe their pre-World War I lives as a mixture of assimilation and distance. Friedrich Solon was nostalgic for the dueling life of the university student, yet he experienced this clichéd bit of German culture as a member of a *Jewish* fraternity, formed in part to counter antisemitism at German universities. Leo Grünebaum remembered growing up in harmony with his gentile neighbors in a village in Hesse, yet recalled that the two groups coexisted without intimacy, and conversion or intermarriage was rare.

Since the task of the writers was to describe their lives in Germany before as well as after 1933, many of them dwelt on the Weimar Republic at length. The double pattern of German-Jewish history, defined by the simultaneity of emancipation and antisemitism, became more sharply accentuated than ever during the Weimar period.[25] On the one hand, Jews had unprecedented success in the medical and legal professions, and individual Jews could take pride in their newly won status–an attitude richly documented in the physicians', lawyers', and judges' contributions to the "My Life in Germany" collection. On the other hand, the traumas of defeat, revolution, and inflation left a residue of vehement antisemitism. In the period of economic and political stabilization from 1924 to 1928, antisemitism retreated to the background, but with the growing world economic crisis and destabilization of the Weimar Republic, it grew again in the late 1920s.[26] An atmosphere of widespread resentment manifest in economic boycotts gave German Jews cause for concern well before the Nazi

[25] Richarz, ed., *Jüdisches Leben in Deutschland*, vol. 3, 13. See also Michael A. Meyer and Michael Brenner, eds., *German-Jewish History in Modern Times*, vol. 4: *Renewal and Destruction, 1918-1945* (New York: Columbia University Press, 1998); Michael Berkowitz, *Western Jewry and the Zionist Project, 1914-1933* (Cambridge and New York: Cambridge University Press, 1997); idem., *The Jewish Self-Image in the West* (New York: New York University Press, 2000); Michael Brenner, *The Renaissance of Jewish Culture in Weimar Germany* (New Haven and London: Yale University Press, 1996); and Trude Maurer, *Ostjuden in Deutschland, 1918-1933* (Hamburg: Christians, 1986).

[26] Ibid., 29.

seizure of power.[27] The writers of the "My Life in Germany" collection, their perceptions sharpened by persecution, often recall how antisemitism heightened toward the end of the Weimar period. Individual experiences varied widely, however. Edith Mann, a music professor, and Mara Oppenheimer, a housewife, were unaware of the squall of hatred forming around them in the later Weimar years. Others were better placed or more alert; even before 1933, physicians such as Martin Andermann and Arthur Samuel encountered open hostility in medical school, and the working-class housewife Martha Neumann noticed the increase in antisemitic street propaganda.

Diverse signs of Jews' standing in German society emerge from the history of Jewish community life, too. Contradictory signs of collective fraying and renewal characterized the decades before 1933. The Jewish population of Germany was in a state of decline in relationship to the German population as a whole, falling from 1.09% in 1880 to 0.76% in 1933. In 1933 there were 503,000 Jews in a total German population of 66,029,000. The demographic decline had numerous causes, including a late average marriage age, effective birth control, and exogamous marriages.[28] As a result of a steady internal migration away from smaller centers of population toward urban settings in which they could expect less antisemitism and greater economic and social opportunity, about a third lived in Berlin, another third in other large cities, while the rest were scattered in small towns and villages.[29]

German Jews supported an organizational life of great diversity before and after 1933. The Central Association of German Citizens of the Jewish Faith (Centralverein deutscher Staatsbürger jüdischen Glaubens), founded in 1893, was the organization most broadly representative of German Jews; liberal and middle-class in its composition and outlook, it had worked to counter antisemitism and to further Jewish acculturation in German society since the nineteenth century, yet not without pride in a distinctive Jewish identity.[30] The Zionist movement held its first formal meeting in Germany

---

[27] Günter Plum, "Wirtschaft und Erwerbsleben," in *Die Juden in Deutschland 1933-1945*, 272.

[28] Kwiet and Eschwege, *Selbstbehauptung und Widerstand*, 50.

[29] Ibid., 53; Richarz, ed., *Jüdisches Leben in Deutschland*, vol. 3, 14-15; Barkai, *From Boycott to Annihilation*, 1.

[30] On the history of the Centralverein before World War I, see Jehuda Reinharz, *Fatherland or Promised Land: The Dilemma of the German Jew, 1893-1914* (Ann Arbor: University of Michigan Press, 1975).

just four years later.[31] After World War I, another major group appeared, the Reich Federation of Jewish Veterans (Reichsbund jüdischer Frontsoldaten). Founded as a defense group against antisemitism, it encouraged Jewish youth to take part in sports and worked to settle Jews in agricultural occupations as ways of "normalizing" Jewish life.[32] Finally, the Jewish Women's League (Jüdischer Frauenbund), founded in 1904, was a middle-class organization that furthered integration into mainstream society, yet also stressed the importance of religious observance.[33]

These voluntary associations are only of moderate importance for the "My Life in Germany" memoirists. One was prominent in the Centralverein (Joseph B. Levy). Several active Zionists contributed memoirs providing insight into the significance of Zionism as a form of cultural self-assertion, if not as a statement of immediate intention to emigrate to Palestine (Kollander, Landau, Zeitlin).[34] There are some memoirs from Jewish community activists too, such as Leo Grünebaum, a religious school teacher in Cologne, and two rabbis, Karl Rosenthal from Berlin and Arthur Blum from Krefeld. Even if they were not active in religious or secular Jewish organizations, other authors used their memoirs as an occasion for rethinking their relationship to Jewish culture.

### *Persecution and Flight*

A half century after they were written, readers may read the memoirs in search of such themes as national and class consciousness, Jewish identity, and political values. But for most writers, the most pressing topic was their experience of persecution and escape from Germany. Jewish accounts often dwelled on the details of how dramatic, public acts of persecution alternated with quieter, continuous acts of harassment until the crescendo of violence

---

[31] Berkowitz, *Zionist Culture and West European Jewry Before the First World War*, and Jehuda Reinharz, ed., *Dokumente zur Geschichte des Deutschen Zionismus 1882-1933* (Tübingen: Mohr, 1981).

[32] Ulrich Dunker, *Der Reichsbund jüdischer Frontsoldaten 1919-1938. Geschichte eines jüdischen Abwehrvereins* (Düsseldorf: Droste, 1977).

[33] Marion A. Kaplan, *The Jewish Feminist Movement in Germany: The Campaigns of the Jüdischer Frauenbund, 1904-1938* (Westport, Conn., and London, England: Greenwood, 1979).

[34] On this theme see Berkowitz, *Zionist Culture and West European Jewry Before the First World War.*

in 1938/39.[35]

Many Germans, Jewish and non-Jewish, initially adopted a wait-and-see attitude toward the new rulers even after events in the spring of 1933 announced the new regime's campaign of theft and violence against German Jews.[36] Nazi street thugs assaulted Jews and ransacked shops in March, and Hitler ordered a one-day boycott of Jewish shops, which took place on April 1. On April 7, the Nazi state promulgated a law aimed at eliminating Jews from civil service.[37] These measures and the persecution of socialists and Communists led to the first wave of refugees from Nazi Germany. At least 37,000 Jews left Germany in 1933 and another 23,000 in 1934 for other parts of Europe, Palestine and the United States, an exodus not equaled until 1938-39.[38]

The collection contains life stories of at least fourteen Jewish emigrés who left in 1933-34. Most were socialists. Some who had thought of emigration to Palestine for some time now made the difficult decision to leave Germany. Few of these early emigrés were people with flourishing businesses or professional practices; Jews with substantial economic interests clung to the hope that Nazi antisemitism would run its course and leave their livelihood intact.

Such hopes became increasingly untenable as the campaign for economic and legal exclusion of Jews from public life mounted in the mid-1930s. The regime improvised new attacks. The so-called Nuremberg legislation of late 1935 forbade marriage between Jews and non-Jews, ordered Jews not to employ female "Aryan" servants, did not allow them to show the national flag, and excluded non-"Aryan" Germans from the category of "citizen" (*Reichsbürger*). It is a measure of the confusion of the times that

[35] For overviews of Nazi policy toward Jews during the 1930s see Karl A. Schleunes, *The Twisted Road to Auschwitz: Nazi Policy Toward German Jews, 1933-1939*, 2nd ed. (Urbana and Chicago: University of Illinois Press, 1990); Uwe Dietrich Adam, *Judenpolitik im Dritten Reich* (Düsseldorf: Droste, 1972); and William Carr, "Nazi Policy Against the Jews," in *Life in the Third Reich*, ed. Richard Bessel (Oxford and New York: Oxford University Press, 1987), 69-82.

[36] See Wolfgang Benz, "Prolog. Der 30. Januar 1933," 15 ff.

[37] The *Gesetz zur Wiederherstellung des Berufsbeamtentums* (Law for the Reestablishment of the Professional Civil Service). Exceptions were made for those who already had civil servant (*Beamter*) status before August 1, 1914, veterans, and those whose fathers or sons had fallen in combat. See Plum, "Wirtschaft und Erwerbleben," 286; cf. Barkai, *From Boycott to Annihilation*, 25-27.

[38] Richarz, *Jüdisches Leben in Deutschland*, vol. 3, 53.

the Nazi leaders themselves argued over how to define who was a Jew.[39] At a moment when government members were unsure of whom they were excluding, ordinary citizens could only guess how much danger they were in: whether partial Jewish ancestry placed them outside the Nazi-defined national community, and even if they were of fully Jewish ancestry, whether the new legislation was a stopping-point or a portent of worse to come. The "My Life in Germany" writers permit us to reconstruct the day-by-day choices of the time and the difficulties of choosing exile. Numerous accounts describe the incidents that finally convinced them to leave; they also contain many reminders of how heavily indifference and opportunism toward Jews outweighed acts of solidarity.[40]

While an atmosphere of intensifying hostility pervades the descriptions of the 1930s, most authors fled only after two culminating events: the Nazi seizure of power (*Anschluss*) in Austria of March 1938 and the collective violence of November 9-10 (*Reichskristallnacht*) of the same year. The memory of these events—or rather, the desire to bear witness to the atrocities the authors had experienced—structures many of the memoirs. As in the preceding years, the persecution of 1938 combined spontaneous popular and planned official violence.[41] In Vienna, Jews were subjected to notorious public humiliations and deported to concentration camps. Ordinary citizens as well as National Socialists stripped Jews of their apartments, houses and businesses even before the newly installed Nazi regime could intervene to funnel Jewish resources into public coffers. This initial anarchy was followed by a succession of legal measures that drastically restricted the number of Jewish university students, established separate Jewish grade and vocational schools, excluded Jews from the free professions, and expropriated Jewish businesses. Adolf Eichmann was put in charge of the office for Jewish emigration from Vienna, which systematically stripped individuals of all their resources before permitting them to leave the country.[42] Almost all the forty

---

[39] Adam, *Judenpolitik im Dritten Reich*, chap.3.

[40] Cf. Barkai, *From Boycott to Annihilation.*

[41] Cf. Karl Dietrich Bracher, *The German Dictatorship: The Origins, Structure, and Effects of National Socialism*, trans. Jean Steinberg (New York: Praeger, 1970), 365.

[42] Gerhard Botz, *Nationalsozialismus in Wien. Machtübernahme und Herrschaftssicherung 1938/39* (Buchloe: DVO, 1988), 10, 95 ff.; Botz, "The Jews of Vienna from the *Anschluss* to the Holocaust," in I. Oxaal, M. Pollak, and G. Bolz, *Jews, Antisemitism and Culture in Vienna* (London and New York: Routledge & Kegan Paul, 1987), 190-194. See also Rudolf Neck and Adam Wandruszka, eds., *Anschluss 1938: Protokoll des Symposiums in Wien am*

accounts of Austrian refugees focus on the sudden disruption of their lives in the spring of 1938. The violent spring in Austria was the prelude to the destruction of November 9-10, in which almost a hundred Jews throughout the enlarged *Reich* were murdered, 7,500 Jewish businesses were ruined, and approximately 30,000 men and women were imprisoned. The Jewish community was then ordered to pay a huge "atonement" tax (*Sühneleistung*) of a billion marks, Jews were required to clean the streets, and their insurance claims were pocketed by the state.[43]

In response to the increasing pressures on their community, Jewish organizations were forced to alter their activities. With Jewish exclusion from economic life, a growing network of self-help organizations had to care for an increasingly impoverished and aging population. Jewish schools and youth organizations grew too as the young were excluded from educational institutions.[44] Ernst Loewenberg describes how the Jewish community of Hamburg prepared young people for emigration to Palestine by providing them with practical education; Sofoni Herz recounts his efforts, as a young man in his early thirties, to protect the children in a Jewish orphanage. Other groups prepared adults for emigration and helped to find sponsors in Great Britain and the United States. Alice Baerwald, who became heavily involved in organizing the emigration of Jews from Danzig to Palestine, testifies to the resourcefulness and energy of one German-Jewish community in response to the persecution of the 1930s.

The events of the *Anschluss* and pogrom convinced most authors, if nothing had done so before, that they could no longer cling to the hope of remaining in Central Europe. Many were imprisoned in concentration camps. On reading through the memoirs, one is struck by their frequent

---

*14. und 15. März 1978* (Munich: Oldenbourg, 1981); Jonny Moser, "Die Entrechtung der Juden im Dritten Reich. Diskriminierung und Terror durch Gesetze, Verordnungen, Erlasse," in *Der Judenprogrom 1938: Von der 'Reichskristallnacht' zum Völkermord* (Frankfurt am Main: Fischer, 1988), 118-131; and Felix Kreissler, ed., *Fünfzig Jahre danach: Der 'Anschluss' von innen und aussen gesehen* (Beiträge zum Internationalen Symposion von Rouen, 29. Februar - 4. März 1988) (Vienna and Zurich: Europaverlag, 1989).

[43] Barkai, *From Boycott to Annihilation*, 133-138.

[44] Yfaat Weiss, *Schicksalsgemeinschaft im Wandel: Jüdische Erziehung im Nationalsozialistischen Deutschland: 1933-1938* (Hamburg: Christians, 1991) esp. 12-41; Richarz, *Jüdisches Leben in Deutschland*, vol.3, 56-58; Barkai, *From Boycott to Annihilation*, 40 ff.; Kaplan, *Jewish Feminist Movement*, 202. The dilemmas of dealing with the Nazi regime also led the most radical German nationalists and Zionists to sorry attempts at compromise— and occasionally collaboration—with the new regime. See Dunker, *Reichsbund*, 132 ff.; and Francis R. Nicosia, "The End of Emancipation and the Illusion of Preferential Treatment: German Zionism, 1933-1938," in *Leo Baeck Institute Year Book* 36 (1991), 243-265.

ability to recall their experiences in Dachau and other camps with precision and objectivity. The memoirs of Fritz Czuska, Schalom Ben Chorin, Stephen W. Jaraz, Fritz Schreier, and Helene Schneider marshal self-restraint to convey the news of a bizarre and inhumane world in the making.

### *Socialists, Communists and Other Outsiders*

Political opponents to the regime form more cohesive groups of memoir writers than do Jews. Their contributions make up approximately ten percent of the collection. Apart from Jews they were the most conspicuous group (represented here, at any rate) to be targeted for Nazi persecution.[45] The quality of the political memoirs in the collection is high, and researchers in search of such sources will find them rewarding.

The "My Life in Germany" memoirs also offer an opportunity to consider socialist and Jewish autobiographies from the *same* moment in time. The attitude of the Nazi leadership toward the organized working class differed in fundamental respects from its attitude toward Jews. Jews were a tiny portion of the population, a convenient focal point for hatred, and a target for economic destruction. The working class was a large portion of the population, it counted with few exceptions as racially "German," and–despite exploitation through overwork and authoritarian management–the regime depended on it for industrial production and preparation for war. The Nazi rulers simultaneously enticed and threatened the working class during the 1930s. By and large workers remained aloof. Unable to challenge the Nazi regime directly, they retreated into the private spheres of family, neighbors and friends.[46]

---

[45] On the repression of working-class organizations, see Martin Broszat, *The Hitler State: The Foundation and Development of the Internal Structure of the Third Reich,* trans. John W. Hiden (London and New York: Longman, 1981), 65-66, 70-72, 81, 85-86; and Bracher, *The German Dictatorship,* 373-378; V.R. Berghahn, *Modern Germany: Society, Economy and Politics in the Twentieth Century* (Cambridge and New York: Cambridge University Press, 1982), 129 ff.; and Gordon Craig, *Germany, 1866-1945* (New York and Oxford: Oxford University Press, 1980), 580-581.

[46] Tim Mason, *Arbeiterklasse und Volksgemeinschaft. Dokumente und Materialien zur deutschen Arbeiterpolitik 1936-1939* (Opladen: Westdeutscher, 1975), esp. 10, 12, 17 ff., 72, 98, 168; Detlev Peukert, *Ruhrarbeiter gegen den Faschismus. Dokumentation über den Widerstand im Ruhrgebiet 1933-1945* (Frankfurt am Main: Röderberg, 1976); Detlev Peukert, *Volksgenossen und Gemeinschaftsfremde. Anpassung, Ausmerze und Aufbegehren unter dem Nationalsozialismus* (Cologne: Bund-Verlag, 1982), 120-171; Hans-Josef Steinberg, *Widerstand und Verfolgung in Essen 1933-1945* (Hanover: Verlag für Literatur und Zeitgeschehen, 1969); Martin Broszat, "Lage der Arbeiterschaft, Arbeiteropposition, Aktivität

If the Nazi treatment of workers in general was cautious, the persecution of labor activists was brutal and swift. Determined to seek revenge on their enemies from the street battles of the twenties and to eliminate a likely source of violent resistance, Nazis quickly rounded up Communist functionaries and persons with prominent connections to the Party, who were beaten, imprisoned, and put in concentration camps.[47] While the regime did not attack Social Democrats with quite the same blanket ferocity, its leaders too ended up in concentration camps or fled into exile.[48]

The memoirs of politically active refugees in the "My Life in Germany" collection contain little evidence of this difference between the fate of Communists and Social Democrats. Class lines define working-class activists and educated functionaries as two distinct groups of memoir writers. There is a special poignancy to the memoirs by workers on the run from the Nazis and still trapped on the European continent (Dudek, Glaser). In seven pages, Martha Lewinsohn offers a brief but illuminating glimpse of the thick network of neighborhoods and friendships that provided some shelter for politically active workers. The Kochs offer contrasting husband-and-wife perspectives, with Hilde Koch recording her own amazing coolness and optimism after her husband's incarceration, a reminder of the personal strengths that made it possible for some individuals to prevail over the trials of persecution and emigration. In such memoirs one sees the day-to-day fortitude of ordinary human beings caught up in an extraordinary struggle, determined to preserve their family and friends and to maintain a socialist

und Verfolgung der illegalen Arbeiterbewegung 1933-1945. Einführung," in *Bayern in der NS-Zeit.,* vol.1: *Soziale Lage und politisches Verhalten der Bevölkerung im Spiegel vertraulicher Berichte,* ed. Martin Broszat, Elke Fröhlich, and Falk Wiesemann (Munich and Vienna, 1977), 200; Broszat, "Resistenz und Widerstand. Eine Zwischenbilanz des Forschungsprojekts," in *Bayern in der NS-Zeit,* vol.4: *Herrschaft und Gesellschaft im Konflikt,* Teil C (Munich and Vienna: Oldenbourg, 1981), 705.

[47] See Horst Duhnke, *Die KPD von 1933 bis 1945* (Cologne: Kiepenheuer und Witsch, 1972); Broszat, "Resistenz und Widerstand," 705, cf. 708; and Hartmut Mehringer, "Die KPD in Bayern 1919-1945. Vorgeschichte, Verfolgung und Widerstand," in *Bayern in der NS-Zeit,* vol.5: *Die Parteien KPD, SPD, BVP in Verfolgung und Widerstand,* ed. Martin Broszat and Hartmut Mehringer (Munich and Vienna: Oldenbourg Verlag, 1983), 66-67, 83, 86-87.

[48] See Patrik von zur Mühlen, "Die SPD zwischen Anpassung und Widerstand," in Jürgen Schmädeke and Peter Steinbach, eds., *Der Widerstand gegen den Nationalsozialismus. Die deutsche Gesellschaft und der Widerstand gegen Hitler* (Munich and Zurich: Piper, 1985), 86-98, esp. 86-89, 91-92, 96-97; and Hartmut Mehringer, "Die Bayerische Sozialdemokratie bis zum Ende des NS-Regimes. Vorgeschichte, Verfolgung und Widerstand," in *Bayern in der NS-Zeit,* vol.5, 287-432, esp. 339, 351-352, and 431-432; and Lewis J. Edinger, *German Exile Politics: The Social Democratic Executive Committee in the Nazi Era* (Berkeley and Los Angeles: University of California Press, 1956).

cultural identity.[49] Some of the socialist activists combine strong professional identity with political commitment. The lawyer James Broh, the physician Käthe Frankenthal, the teacher Heinrich Kromayer, and the educator Anna Siemsen all write about their lives with an incisive blend of insights derived from a professional community and from their passionate engagement in the politics of the period.

These socialists, in contrast to less politicized refugees, were usually able to distance themselves from what National Socialism had made of German society. After all, there was a high degree of ongoing rationality to their experience. Their exile was *political*; it was the outcome of voluntary commitments, and while no one anticipated the full force of the assault, it came as no surprise that they were under attack from a radical right-wing regime. The Nazis were not able to take away their national identity, for their understanding of "Germany" had grown out of a hardy democratic culture, and they felt themselves to be the authentic bearers of German values. Whether Jewish (Broh, Frankenthal) or Protestant (Siemsen, Kromayer), these autobiographers underwent an abrupt and painful loss of social and professional status that contrasts with the experience of apolitical Jewish professionals. At least intellectually and politically, they had come to terms with their exile.

While socialists and Communists make up the largest group of politically active refugees, individuals with other affiliations, too, contributed to the collection.[50] Otto Thieme, a theologian and member of the Confessing Church, found himself at odds with the authorities early on, as did Kuno Fiedler, who narrates in great detail his differences with the reactionary policies of the Protestant Church.[51] There are also a few memoirs by liberal

---

[49] Cf. Elke Fröhlich, *Die Herausforderung des Einzelnen*, ch. 1, "Zwei Münchner Kommunisten," esp. 48.

[50] On the varieties of opposition and dissent, see Klaus-Jürgen Müller and Hans Mommsen, "Der deutsche Widerstand gegen das NS-Regime. Zur Historiographie des Widerstandes," in *Der deutsche Widerstand 1933-1945*, ed. Klaus-Jürgen Müller (Paderborn: Schoning, 1986), 13-21; cf. the contributions to Schmädeke and Steinbach, eds., *Der Widerstand gegen den Nationalsozialismus. Die deutsche Gesellschaft und der Widerstand gegen Hitler* (Munich: R. Piper, 1985).

[51] For general orientation on religious opposition to the Nazi regime, see Günther van Norden, "Zwischen Kooperation und Teilwiderstand: Die Rolle der Kirchen und Konfessionen - Ein Überblick über Forschungspositionen," in Schmädeke und Steinbach, eds., *Der Widerstand gegen den Nationalsozialismus*, 227-239, esp. 228; and Klaus Scholder, *The Churches and the Third Reich*, vol.1: *Preliminary History and the Time of Illusions 1918-1934* (Philadelphia: Fortress Press, 1988), esp. 187 and 279. See also Friedrich Wilhelm Graf, "Der Weimarer Barth – ein linker Liberaler?," in *Evangelische Theologie* 47 (Nov.-Dec. 1987), 555-566, esp. 556-558. On the Protestant Church and dissent, see Günther van Norden, "Widerstand im deutschen Protestantismus 1933-1945," in Müller, ed., *Der deutsche*

opponents of the regime, including Constance Hallgarten's evocation of her *grand bourgeois* milieu in Munich and activities as an activist for feminism and world peace, and Otto Lehmann's description of pacifist circles. In other cases quirks of fate and character set individuals at odds with the regime, voluntarily or involuntarily. Bruno Gebhard, a public health official originally imbued with the conservative mentality of an upper-class physician, regained his political sanity by visiting the United States and realizing how far Germany had slipped into collective madness; Maria Kahle, who did not hesitate to help her Jewish neighbors under attack in 1938, turned herself into an outcast.

### *Professional Loyalties*

To late twentieth-century observers, the Nazi era is above all associated with the systematic atrocities of the death camps of the 1940s, machines for the physical and spiritual destruction of the regime's victims. The "My Life in Germany" memoirists take us back to an earlier and different moment. Their continuity with their pre-1933 lives was perceptibly greater. Although hardly indifferent to the surrounding violence, they continued to feel a strong sense of affinity with their work and often organized their narratives around their occupational fate. Their writing styles too, were often closely tied to their form of work; authors from the liberal professions often exercised the habits of analytical observation acquired in their education and professional practice. Writers and journalists brought self-conscious literary craft to their memoirs. Occupational life provided a setting in which one could view just how the state impinged on everyday lives and how dealings with colleagues, clients, and customers changed before and after 1933.

OCCUPATIONS OF ESSAY WRITERS

| | |
|---|---|
| lawyers, judges | 33 |
| (lawyers: | 30) |
| teachers, professors | 28 |

*Widerstand*, 108-134, esp. 109, 130-134; Gerhard Besier, "Ansätze zum politischen Widerstand in der Bekennenden Kirche. Zur gegenwärtigen Forschungslage," in Schmädeke and Steinbach, eds., *Der Widerstand gegen den Nationalsozialismus*, 265-280, esp. 267; and Eberhard Bethge, "Zwischen Bekenntnis und Widerstand: Erfahrungen in der Altpreussischen Union," in ibid., 281-313, esp. 291.

| | |
|---|---|
| writers, journalists, translators | 31 |
| indep. businesspeople, manufacturers | 26 |
| physicians and dentists | 24 |
| sales clerks, office workers* | 16 |
| housewives* | 12 |
| managers | 8 |
| students | 9 |
| workers (skilled) | 9 |
| actors/painters | 8 |
| rabbis and ministers | 5 |
| architects/engineers | 5 |
| social workers* | 3 |
| Other** | 8 |

* majority female

** nurse, photographer, scientist, textile designer, political activist (2), dog trainer, horse trainer.

Jews in different occupations faced different forms of persecution. German Jews played a prominent role in running small and medium-sized businesses in the retail and wholesale trades; in 1933 over sixty percent of all gainfully employed Jews were active in some form of business. At the modest end of the business classes, Jewish peddlers were visible targets and were often driven from their market stalls as early as 1933. Willy Bornstein, a traveling salesman and exhibitor at fairs and carnivals, reports close encounters with Nazis well before then. No longer able to support his family, by the mid-1930s he had fled with them to Belgium.

Owners of more stable small and medium-sized businesses were only slightly better off. They too were visible targets as soon as the Nazis came to power. The "My Life in Germany" memoirs testify to the boycotts and harassment facing the owners of small businesses: Hans Kosterliz, manager of a store in Breslau, Ida Lohr, owner of a glove store in Munich, and Albert Sorkin, a grocer in Freiburg, report on the threats to their livelihoods. Rural Jews such as Friedrich Weil also faced pressure to abandon their trades.[52]

Alongside dramatic but unpredictable public attacks, the Nazi regime quickly instituted a less obvious but persistent draining of Jewish resources.

[52] See also the reports by Karl Schwabe and Edwin Landau, who were less disturbed by events in the early years. Some farmers continued to rely on Jewish merchants and resisted Nazi attempts to discourage them; see Plum, "Wirtschaft und Erwerbsleben," 297-304.

Even before the November pogrom of 1938, an accelerated series of laws eliminated Jews from most areas of the economy and steered Jewish assets into the coffers of the Nazi state. By a law of April 1938, Jews were required to make a declaration of their assets; in June, the definition of a "Jewish" business concern was stipulated. These laws prepared the way for seizing the resources of all Jewish businesses, including wholesale and manufacturing firms that had hitherto managed to avoid being shaken down.[53] The manufacturer Eugen Federlein reports in his memoir that his manufacturing business continued with little interference until 1938. By May 1939 the destruction of Jewish property and livelihoods had advanced so far that only 15.6 percent out of a total of 214,000 remaining Jews were still gainfully employed.[54]

The businessmen and women who contributed memoirs, then, wrote under the impact of direct violence and creeping bureaucratic theft. Their narratives lack the literary and analytical skill of many of the memoirs by lawyers, teachers, and other professionals trained in social observation and more accustomed to expressing themselves in writing. Yet their stories offer insight into the situation of the majority of German Jews dependent on some form of commercial activity. From the wealthy manufacturer "Aralk" to the small trader such as Bornstein, from the department store owner Karl Schwabe to the wine dealer Friedrich Weil, the business memoirists exemplify the struggle of thousands of Jews to survive day-to-day harassment.

Jews entered different branches of the legal system in impressive numbers in the late nineteenth and early twentieth centuries: from the 1880s to 1904, the Jewish percentage of Prussian attorneys rose from 7.3 percent to 27.4 percent.[55] Jewish attorneys in civil service or academic positions were quite rare until after World War I, however. It was only during the Weimar Republic that Jews were permitted to serve in large numbers as judges and as notaries.[56] They also gained positions of public prestige within legal profession in the 1920s; eleven out of the twenty-five board members of the German Lawyers Association (*Deutscher Anwaltverein*) were Jewish in 1933,

[53] The few larger factories owned by Jews had remained largely undisturbed until then; ibid., 304-305.

[54] Barkai, *From Boycott to Annihilation*, 119 ff., 153-154.

[55] Konrad H. Jarausch, "Jewish Lawyers in Germany, 1848-1938: The Disintegration of a Profession," in *Leo Baeck Institute Year Book* 36 (1991), 174.

[56] Only 2.82 percent of the judges in Prussia were Jewish in 1914. Ibid.

as was the editor of the *Juristische Wochenschrift*.[57] Non-Jewish clients and colleagues seem increasingly to have accepted the prominence of Jews in the legal world. At the same time Jewish success stirred widespread resentment on the radical right, making members of the legal professions one of the chief targets of antisemitic resentment.[58]

The manuscripts in the collection suggest how difficult it was for Jews, even in the Weimar Republic, to receive state employment. Only four writers with a legal education worked in the civil service, and among them Alfred Christian Oppler was, by any but a Nazi definition, a Protestant. (He actually joined the National Socialist Party in 1933, only to be dismissed from the civil service in 1936.) Another, Fritz Goldschmidt, became a judge because he felt that an academic career was not open to him (cf. Mannes, Steinfels). Twenty-eight were lawyers with independent practices or, in a few cases, in-house business attorneys; especially noteworthy are Karl Friedländer's observations, from the standpoint of a counselor to an industrial firm, on the transformation of the legal system. Two leftist lawyers–James Broh, a defender of socialists and Communists, and Max Hirschberg, also active in political cases–come alive in the memoirs not as victims, but as impassioned citizens with keen powers of political analysis. Others offer valuable comments on the decline of democracy in Germany in their hometowns (Bing, Marcus, Neumann, Nord, Polke). Many of these lawyers were exercised in an indirect civic vocation through their legal calling.

Medicine, like law, was a profession in which antisemitism trailed Jewish achievement during the Weimar Republic. The background to the sinister attacks on Jewish doctors after World War I was an employment crisis within the medical profession. Because of the large oversupply of physicians, new graduates had to endure frustrating waiting periods in order to become established practitioners. Jews entered the medical profession in disproportionate numbers, and at the end of the Weimar Republic, some ten percent of the physicians in Germany were Jewish.[59] Non-Jewish physicians were

---

[57] Jarausch, "Disintegration of a Profession," 175-177.

[58] Jarausch, "Disintegration of a Profession," 177-178. On political attitudes in the legal profession, see also Ralph Angermund, "Die geprellten 'Richterkönige'. Zum Niedergang der Justiz im NS-Staat," 304-342; and Axel Azzola, "Die rechtliche Ausschaltung der Juden aus dem öffentlichen Leben im Jahre 1933. Ein Beitrag zur Vorgeschichte eines Genozids," 104-117, in Ralf Dreier and Wolfgang Sellert, eds., *Recht und Justiz im 'Dritten Reich'* (Frankfurt am Main: Suhrkamp, 1989).

[59] Geoffrey Cocks, "Partners and Pariahs: Jews and Medicine in Modern German Society," *Leo Baeck Institute Year Book* 36 (1991), 195.

disproportionately attracted to right-wing radicalism even before 1933. About 40% of the non-Jewish doctors in Germany were active in Nazi organizations after Hitler's seizure of power.[60] They spurred local officials to enact discriminatory legislation against Jewish doctors even before the national regime acted. A relentless campaign of terror and legal harassment followed the Nazi seizure of power, culminating in complete decertification of Jewish doctors in the fall of 1938.[61]

The accounts of the twenty-four physicians and dentists include material on education, scientific and professional ethos, the juxtaposition of integration and prejudice in the Weimar period, and the day-by-day unfolding of persecution after 1933. Like the doctors' memoirs they reveal the complex shadings of German-Jewish identity in the first four decades of the twentieth century: some of the doctors were from Orthodox religious backgrounds (Mibberlin, Neustaetter); some were attracted to Zionism (Kretschmar, Mibberlin); some by birth or social standing felt solidly at home in Germany's *Bürgertum* (Necheles-Magnus, Samuel, R. Wolf, Frankenthal); some became socialists (Frankenthal, Nathorff). In contrast to the exclusively male lawyers' collection, several of the doctors' manuscripts are by women (Frankenthal, Nathorff, Necheles-Magnus, Tobias). While the lawyers offer more insight into the civic life of the Weimar Republic, the doctors have more to say about day-to-day personal relationships, which they observed at close range in private practices, hospitals and clinics.

While members of the liberal professions and business classes form the largest groups of "My Life in Germany" memoirists, writers and teachers are also numerous. Teachers form a heterogeneous category in the collection. The well-known philosopher Karl Löwith contributed a memoir (with an acerbic portrait of Martin Heidegger), as did the spouses of two professors with international reputations, Ernst Kahle and George Hallgarten. Other memoirs lead into the world of vocational schooling (Kromayer), the Gymnasium (Klugmann, Löwenberg, Spiegel), Jewish education (Grünebaum, Herz, Levy), and teachers' education (Mann, Siemsen). The collection also contains narratives by high school students (Scherzer, Stein, Spiegel). Nazi *Gleichschaltung* affected educators from all sorts of different religious and ideological backgrounds. Karl Löwith, secularized but of Jewish ancestry, the mathematician Robert Breusch, who was engaged to a Jewish woman,

[60] See Michael H. Kater, "Professionalization and Socialization of Physicians in Wilhelmine and Weimar Germany," in *Journal of Contemporary History*, vol. 20 (1985), 689-693; and idem., *Doctors under Hitler* (Chapel Hill and London, 1989).

[61] Kater, *Doctors under Hitler*, 183 ff., 200.

Theodoro Wilhelm, a dissident Catholic youth worker, and Karl Otto Thieme, a theology professor and member of the Confessing Church, and Kuno Fiedler, a dissident Protestant minister and public school teacher, made themselves unacceptable to the Nazi regime. All of the teachers represented in the "My Life in Germany" collection had lost their jobs by 1935. Their memoirs offer a different perspective from that of the now-celebrated diaries of Victor Klemperer, a Jewish professor of Romance languages in Dresden who survived the entire war in Germany (and continued afterwards to teach in the German Democratic Republic). Klemperer's diaries, which became a German best-seller after their publication in 1995, give the reader the sensation of being pulled into the Third Reich; they are the private testimony of a man who despite the most obvious dangers could not bring himself to leave.[62] The "My Life in Germany" teachers' memoirs have a palpably different relationship to Germany, for their authors did emigrate, they self-consciously addressed an American audience, and they had a correspondingly greater psychological distance from German society.

Writers, journalists, and translators are another heterogeneous group of "professionals" among the memoir writers. Memoirists with no previous experience sometimes adopted the occupational classification "writer," perhaps as a way to establish themselves abroad. But also represented are novelists (Rathgeber, Rie) and established journalists and editors (Reiner, Gyssling).[63] The detailed and well-written accounts of those men and women reporting on their days as political newswriters in the 1920s and 1930s are still fascinating to read. Others, such as David Bach and Carl Paeschke, write detailed descriptions of the subculture of socialist journalism. With their professional reporting skills, Raoul Auernheimer and Schalom Ben-Chorin are especially effective chroniclers of concentration camp experiences. It seems surprising in retrospect that only one of the journalists, Henry Katz, published his memoirs at the time in the United States, perhaps evidence of the difficulty of getting into print in a foreign literary world.[64]

---

[62] Klemperer, *I Will Bear Witness.*

[63] On Gyssling, see Leonidas E. Hill, "Walter Gyssling, the Centralverein and the Büro Wilhelmstrasse, 1929-1933," *Leo Baeck Institute Yearbook* 38 (1993), 193-208; ibid., 193, 200, gives the date of Gyssling's death (1980), which we have cited in the catalogue portion of the present work.

[64] H.W. Katz, *No.21 Castle St*, trans. Norbert Guterman (New York: Viking, 1940). German publication: H.W. Katz, *Schlossgasse 21: In einer kleinen deutschen Stadt* (Weinheim: Beltz Quadriga, 1994). Correspondence in the file indicates that the Harvard professors encouraged publication and made contacts for the manuscript with American publishers.

Some of the most interesting memoirs come from outside conventional professional categories. Max Geffner relates how, despite his blindness, he is able to complete his doctorate in German literature and to go on to a career as teacher to the blind and collector of Braille books; "John Hay" (a pseudonym) recalls the political transformation of the Berlin theater world of the 1920s and 1930s; the grocer Felix Sorkin describes his life among the competitive chess players of Weimar Germany; Rudolfine Menzel discusses the world of dog breeders and dog trainers. Like many others in the collection, these memoirists did not have a strong Jewish or political identity, but identified rather with a particular vocation or social environment. To write about them simply as Jews or political opponents of the regime without further qualification, or to typecast them as Jews (assimilated, religious, Zionist, etc.) would be to distort or deny their self-image. At the same time they remind us of the extraordinary variety of Jewish life in the inter-war years, impossible to imagine without attention to individuals.

### *Women as Memoirists*

Approximately sixty-seven entries, over 25% of the total retained in the collection, were written by women.[65] They represent a wide range of social types, including wealthy and working-class women, Jews and non-Jews, professionals and housewives.[66] Only a few were prominent in public life (Frankenthal, Siemsen, Hallgarten). Many others, however, had some kind of professional education (conforming to the general pattern of a higher level of education among Jewish than among non-Jewish women in Weimar Germany) and work experiences outside the home. Women memoirists, like their male counterparts, were barred from their jobs or subject to harassment that made their work situations unbearable after 1933. Others were directly involved as assistants in the business or professional practice of their husbands and described the shared effects of Nazi persecution on their livelihood (Albersheim, Lohr, Popper).

Women also fulfilled traditional female roles. As mothers, wives and daughters they did much of the "emotional labor" for their families. Many of

[65] The exact number is uncertain. There are seventy-three authors identified as female, but for eight of them there is neither a manuscript nor biographical data.

[66] One group not discussed on the following pages is the thirteen American women contributors. Some had emigrated decades earlier (or were children of German immigrants to the US) and returned for a stay in the 1930s. A few are sympathetic to the Nazi state (Kessel, Kekone). Others, such as Elsie Axelrath, Miriam Arrington, and Hilda Honnet Sichel, were Americans who married German men and lived in Germany at some point during the 1920s and early 1930s.

their memoirs emphasized the impact of Nazi persecution on personal relationships.[67] Women had to care for unemployed husbands and harassed children, find new homes after being forced out of old ones, and maintain networks of friends and neighbors. Maria Kahle, a Catholic, discusses the Nazis' ideological assault on her husband and children; Annemarie Wolfram and Elisabeth Drexler relate the effects of persecution on Jewish families. In addition to the ever more difficult tasks of providing food and shelter, women frequently took on the responsibility of arranging for emigration.[68] Since men were often released from concentration camp on the condition that that they emigrate as soon as possible, women's activism in securing passports and visas could be essential for survival. Many of the women's memoirs describe their struggle to secure the release of their husbands and their preparations for emigration.

Not all stories were family dramas; a few of the female writers were involved in the Jewish community's collective aid and emigration efforts. Since the Wilhelmine era, German-Jewish women had been highly active organizers for social reform and heightened Jewish cultural awareness.[69] After 1933 Jewish women helped to prepare the young for emigration, to create alternative schools for Jewish children inside Germany, and to provide for the poor and elderly. Alice Baerwald and Hannah Bernheim exemplify how after 1933 Jewish women often became more active in Jewish self-help organizations than before. Many of the women's memoirs in the "My Life in Germany Collection" document the power of the Nazi regime to isolate its citizens; these memoirists of community self-help are a reminder of how effectively cooperation could further survival and bolster morale.[70]

While some Jewish women were able to cope with their increasing isolation from mainstream life by forging bonds of solidarity and friendship within the Jewish community, such an alternative was not open to those non-Jewish women who were persecuted because of their marriage to or

[67] Sixty percent of the women who submitted memoirs were childless, and approximately a quarter were single or divorced.

[68] Cf. Marion Kaplan, "Jewish Women in Nazi Germany: Daily Life, Daily Struggles, 1933-1939," in *Juden in Deutschland. Emanzipation, Integration, Verfolgung und Vernichtung*, ed. Peter Freimark, Alice Jankowski, and Ina S. Lorenz (Hamburg: Christians, 1991), 419 ff.

[69] Kaplan, "Jewish Women in Nazi Germany," 408-409; Kaplan, *The Jewish Feminist Movement*.

[70] Sybil Milton, "Women and the Holocaust: the Case of German and German-Jewish Women," in: *When Biology Became Destiny: Women in Weimar and Nazi Germany*, ed. Renate Bridenthal, Atina Grossmann and Marion Kaplan (New York 1984), 297-302, 317-322.

friendship with Jewish men. Most of these women relate that they did not give much thought before 1933 to the "mixed" character of their marriage. As the Nazis fused national and racial identity, these women became the embodiment of an unpardonable transgression. Women such as Verena Hellwig, Hildegard Bollmann and Eva Wysbar were unprepared to cope with their sudden status as outcasts, and their memoirs highlight the enormous pressures on women to dissolve relationships and marriages. Their stories illustrate the abrupt shift from an open society to an oppressive and vengeful one.[71]

### *Conclusion: Public Categories and Personal Identities*

Their unified date of composition in 1939/1940 makes the "My Life in Germany" memoirs not just individual testimonies, but a collective montage. The immediacy of the dangers they had survived and the fact that many writers found themselves in the midst of a widening world conflict as they set down their stories contribute to the ensemble's thematic cohesion. There is a retrospective danger of accepting the categories of the Third Reich as a *fait accompli*–and in particular of viewing "Germans" and "Jews" as separate entities. This is not the standpoint of the memoirs. They permit us to view these lives from the inside, demonstrating how the authors were never just Jews, or socialists, or dissidents. Rather, they belonged to overlapping social circles, each of which contributed to the formation of a many-sided personal identity.[72] The variety and complexity of the memoirs not only contradicts the caricatures of the Nazi regime, but also reminds us of the complexity of German society before 1933.

The memoirs of the "My Life in Germany" collection also add a wealth of valuable evidence to discussion of the types of dissidence in German society, for they contain innumerable everyday examples of persistence,

[71] Of the forty-two Jewish women writers only one was married to a non-Jew. Five out of sixteen non-Jewish women writers were married to Jews and two to "half-Jewish" men. The collection also contains four memoirs of non-Jewish men who married Jewish women (Breusch, Diel, Kromayer and Schwartzert). In most cases these men married only after leaving Germany with their future wives. Cf. Nathan Stoltzfus, *Resistance of the Heart: Intermarriage and the Rosenstrasse Protest in Nazi Germany* (New York and London: Norton, 1996).

[72] Cf. Georg Simmel, "Die Kreuzung sozialer Kreise," in *Soziologie. Untersuchungen über die Formen der Vergesellschaftung* (1908; Berlin, 1968), 305-344.

courage, and chutzpah.[73] At the same time the manuscripts are a caution against expecting duress to bring out the "best" in people, a reminder that moral mediocrity and opportunism, common enough under ordinary circumstances, flourish under dictatorship. The freshness of the experiences contributed to a certain frankness in the manuscripts: authors were at times naive about relating their own responses to the regime and uninhibited about sharing their indignation over disappointments and betrayals. The varieties of persecution and collaboration, too, emerge from the collection. From the beginning of the Nazi regime, the authors faced harassment by schoolmates, neighbors, and colleagues; bureaucrats stripped them of their livelihood and threw hurdles in their way while demanding that they leave the country; street assaults and concentration camps threatened their physical survival. The picture of Germans that emerges from these hundreds of manuscripts is not a pretty one. The overwhelming reality facing the authors was not German society's misgivings toward the regime or gestures of solidarity, but the collaboration of regime and populace.[74]

Compared to the millions who perished in the Holocaust, many of the "My Life in Germany" participants could narrate their lives as a success story. They had come through their experience of persecution dignified and often eloquent. The experience of the ones who were able to settle in the United States or another safe haven was exceptional. Nonetheless they greatly expand our knowledge of how individuals responded to an all-enveloping tyranny. The capacity for self-assertion was typically strongest among those who had developed a sustaining religious or political credo—such as traditional religious belief, Zionism, or socialism—or who (like socialist workers) had links to a community that could provide resources for survival and sustain morale. Most of the memoirists, however, had to assert themselves in Germany and make their way to freedom on their own. Maintaining their humanity did not end with emigration; the very act of sending in their manuscripts was in its own right an important act of self-assertion. Through their writings, their lives in Germany still come to life for readers today.

---

[73] Cf. Martin Broszat, "Resistenz und Widerstand. Eine Zwischenbilanz des Forschungsprojekts," in *Bayern in der NS-Zeit*, vol.4: *Herrschaft und Gesellschaft im Konflikte*, Teil C (Munich and Vienna, 1981), 692-693, 697-698; Fröhlich, *Die Herausforderung des Einzelnen*, 22; Kershaw, *Popular Opinion and Political Dissent*, vii, 2-3.

[74] Cf. the critique of the literature on dissidence in Peter Fritzsche, "Where Did All the Nazis Go? Reflections on Resistance and Collaboration," in *Tel Aviver Jahrbuch für deutsche Geschichte* 23 (1994), 191-214.

# PART II:

# CATALOGUE

The following catalogue lists all files of the "My Life in Germany" collection preserved in Houghton Library, Harvard University. Houghton Library has an alphabetical and numbered index to the collection, which we have used as the basis for our own sequential listing.[1] The numbers assigned to the entries by the Houghton are used throughout our catalogue and index. The names on the files are also reproduced here in the spelling used by the Houghton Library (i.e., without umlauts). Our index, however, uses umlauts in keeping with standard German orthography.

Entries are present in Houghton either in original manuscript or in microfilm form, and they vary greatly in length and physical quality. We have noted the page length of each available catalogue entry, but this only roughly indicates the length of the manuscript, since page size varies widely from notebook-size pages covered in large handwriting to single-spaced typed pages. Some entries are difficult to read because of poor paper or poor handwriting (or both). Some of the microfilmed entries are barely legible; the author's name is not always clearly identified on the film. We have noted whether entries are missing, preserved in the original form, or available on microfilm.

Many files contain materials besides the entry itself. Most frequent is routine correspondence such as a cover letter by the writer and a letter of acknowledgment by the Harvard recipients. We have only noted correspondence when it contains important information about the writer of the essay. Files also sometimes contain evaluations, supplementary materials sent by the essay writers, and notes about prizes awards. We have indicated the presence of such materials. In some cases no entry has been preserved at all in the collection. When this was the case we tried to reconstruct the

---

[1] The Houghton call number for the collection is bMS Ger 91. The collection has been at Houghton since 1958, when it was given by Sidney Fay. Letter from Dr. Leslie A. Morris, Curator of Manuscripts, Houghton Library, to Harry Liebersohn, 28 Feb. 1995.

Our catalogue lists only the files in the Houghton collection. It does not list competition entries that were not listed as a Houghton file and were eventually housed elsewhere. In particular it does not include a number of memoirs entitled "Mein Leben in Deutschland vor und nach dem 30. Januar 1933" or any other competition manuscripts that are housed and indexed only in the Leo Baeck Institute, New York. We found five memoirs there by this title whose authors do not appear in the Houghton Library index.

essay's contents from evaluations if they were present.

In response to the Harvard organizers' request in their announcement of the competition, most memoirists sent in basic biographical data about themselves. When this data was insufficient or the entry was missing, we have drawn on the following other sources for factual materials: evaluations in the files; the catalogue of the Leo Baeck Institute, New York (LBI); *National Union Catalogue*, 1956, 1964, and 1968 editions (NUC); *Gesamtverzeichnis des Deutschsprachigen Schrifttums*, 1911-1965 (Munich, 1976-1981). (GV); *Biographisches Handbuch der deutschsprachigen Emigration nach 1933*, ed. Werner Röder and Herbert A. Strauss (Munich and New York, 1980-1983) (Röder/Strauss); and Leonidas E. Hill, "Walter Gyssling, the Centralverein and the Büro Wilhelmstrasse, 1929-1933," *Leo Baeck Institute Yearbook* 38 (1993), 193-208.

The following collections contain excerpts of "My Life in Germany" memoirs and have been cited in the catalogue: Margarete Limberg and Hubert Rübsaat, eds., *Sie durften nicht mehr Deutsche sein. Jüdischer Alltag in Deutschland 1933-1938* (Frankfurt, 1990); Andreas Lixl-Purcell, ed., *Women of Exile: German-Jewish Autobiographies since 1933* (New York, 1988); Monika Richarz, ed., *Jüdisches Leben in Deutschland*, vol. 2: *Selbstzeugnisse zur Sozialgeschichte im Kaiserreich* (Stuttgart, 1979); and ibid., vol. 3: *Selbstzeugnisse zur Sozialgeschichte, 1918-1945* (Stuttgart, 1982).

Abbreviated sample entries:

134. Levi, Julius Walter; [b. Oct. 9, 1891 in Munich, physician,][2] writer, humorist; 1940: New York City.

The file contains only correspondence and an evaluation.

The evaluation states that it was the most humorous entry. The manuscript was returned to the author in 1961 at his request.

Manuscript original at the LBI.[3]

2 Information from the sources cited at the end of the entry.

3 Location of manuscript original or copies outside Houghton library.

Lit.: NUC. Papers: LBI.[4]

137.[5] **Lewinsohn, Martha**; 39[6]; m.[7], ch: 1 (son)[8]; housewife (husband: electrician)[9]; last German residence: Dresden,[10] 1939: Copenhagen, 1940: Visby/Sweden[11]

7 pp., typescript, evaluation.[12]

---

[4] Location of personal papers.

[5] File number in the Houghton Library index.

[6] Age at the time the entry was sent.

[7] Married (or other family status; s = single).

[8] Number and sex of children.

[9] Occupation, usually the last occupation before emigration; sometimes more than one occupation is supplied if important for the autobiography; for female authors, former occupation and their husband's former occupation.

[10] Last German residence before emigration; "Germany" includes Austria after March 1938.

[11] Residence at the time the entry was written or sent; sometimes place of residence changed between 1939 and 1941, in which case more than one residence is listed.

[12] Contents of file: number of pages, manuscript form, and evaluation if present.

1. Abraham, Georg; 34, b: Provinz Bromberg; Jewish, m; wholesale agent to tobacco manufacturers; last German residence: Bromberg/East Prussia, 1940: Camp Kitchener/Somerset, England.

The author is the son of a craftsman but grows up in an orphanage after World War I and is educated in a *Volksschule*. He successfully rises to the position of an independent wholesale agent with eight employees. The memoir also describes the author's arrest, incarceration in a concentration camp, and emigration to England.

21 pp., typescript, evaluation.

2. Ahronheim, Charles; b: May 26, 1875, Berlin; Jewish, m, (Hanna Schalit) ch: 2 (sons); physician; last German residence: Berlin, 1940: Jackson/Michigan.

The author describes his education as a young dermatologist at a university hospital and as a ship doctor. He settles in Palestine, but leaves to open up a private practice in Dusseldorf and later Berlin, where he practices from 1919 until 1935. He is arrested and put into a concentration camp, but manages to leave for the United States in 1935, where he joins his two adult sons.

40 pp., typescript (on microfilm), evaluation.

3. Albersheim, Erna; b: 1892, New York City; Protestant (father Protestant, mother Jewish), w; businesswoman, ch: 1 (daughter); last German residence: Frankfurt am Main, 1940: Richmond/Virginia.

The American-born author moves to Germany in 1914 after her marriage to a German owner of a cosmetics and perfume business. The memoir describes the difficult years of World War I and the political events of the Weimar years from the perspective of an upper-class member of Frankfurt's Jewish community. Much of the account deals with the difficulties of continuing the business under the Nazis after her husband's death in 1932. The business is finally sold, and Albersheim leaves with her daughter in

January 1939. The somewhat confused and discontinuous narrative contains a great deal of information on daily life and harassments under the Nazis.

75 pp., typescript, in English, evaluation.

4. **Albert, Henry**; b: 1913, Austria; Catholic, later Jewish (father Jewish convert, mother Catholic); university student, reserve officer.

The manuscript was returned to the author and was not microfilmed. The file contains an evaluation, with extensive quotes from the manuscript, of antisemitism and life in Austria before and after the *Anschluss.*

Over 50 pp., evaluation.

5. **Altmann, Eugen**; b: 1876, Gumbinnen/East Prussia; Jewish, m, ch: 2; wholesale merchant in the garment industry; last German residence: Breslau, 1940: San Francisco/California.

This literate memoir describes a solid middle-class existence before World War I. The author leaves Gymnasium at age sixteen to begin an apprenticeship in the garment industry. His account focuses on the relationships between people of different class backgrounds and between Jews and non-Jews, especially in the garment business. After a friend's warning he leaves before November 1938.

53 pp., typescript.

6. **Andermann, Martin**; 35, b: Königsberg; Jewish, m; physician; last German residence: Königsberg, 1940: Buffalo/New York.

The author describes the Königsberg of his youth and his upbringing in a liberal Jewish family. While a young medical student he becomes an admirer of Heideggger and Husserl; the memoir also recalls the Social Democrats and their culture in Berlin during the 1920s. Insightful, too, are the discussions of Jews in the medical profession and the author's experiences with antisemitism and National Socialist beliefs among his colleagues at the university hospital in Heidelberg.

119 pp., typescript, evaluation.

Lit: Limberg/Rübsaat.

7. **Apothaker, Harry**; 49; Jewish, m; operator in electrical plant; last German residence: ?, 1940: Atlantic City/New Jersey.

A working-class American of German-Jewish background, the author recounts his experiences as an American soldier in Germany during and after World War I in brief anecdotes.

3 pp., typescript, in English.

8. **"Aralk"** (pseudonym); 44; Jewish, m, ch: 3; housewife, (husband: factory owner); last German residence: Munich, 1940: Detroit/Michigan.

The author comes from a well-to-do family of Munich wholesale merchants and marries a wealthy industrialist. Her well-organized and detailed memoir describes the years during and after World War I from the perspective of an upper-class businessman's wife. Inflation and political uncertainties of the Weimar years are discussed, as are the effects of the Nazi seizure of power on her family and the family business. With considerable effort, she and her family finally secure immigration visas to the United States.

85 pp., typescript, evaluation.

Lit.: Limberg/Rübsaat.

9. **Arrington, Miriam**; 32, b: Montgomery/Alabama; m; English teacher (husband: lawyer); last German residence: Vienna, 1940: Montgomery/Alabama.

In her engagingly written, witty memoir the author tells about her marriage to a young Austrian lawyer, whom she meets during a European tour. Living in Vienna from 1928 until she separates from her husband and leaves in 1939, she observes the gradual transformation of Austrian society—and her husband—by the Nazi movement.

89 pp., typescript, in English.

10. **Auernheimer, Raoul**; b: April 15, 1876, Vienna [d. Jan.7, 1948, Oakland/CA]; Protestant, m; writer; last German residence: Vienna, 1940: New York City, 1941: California.

A well-known Viennese author of several novels and essays, Auernheimer submitted not a memoir, but a detailed account of his experiences at the Dachau concentration camp, entitled "Arbeit Macht Frei". No publication of the manuscript is known.

134 pp., typescript, on microfilm.

Lit.: NUC, GV, Roeder/Strauss; personal papers: University of California/Riverside and LBI.

11. **Aust, Joseph**; 26, b: Silesia; Catholic; confectioner; last German residence: Hamburg, 1940: British internment camp in Devonshire.

A cook aboard merchant marine ships, the author describes his involvement in the early Nazi movement. The memoir gives a detailed account of a small-town Nazi who, disturbed by big city life and a perceived lack of discipline in politics, sees a better future under Hitler.

34 pp., handwritten.

12. **Axelrath, Elsie**; 39, b: U.S.; Jewish, m, ch: 1 (daughter), housewife (husband: representative of U.S. company in Germany); last German residence: Hamburg, 1940: Woodmere/Long Island.

The wife of an American businessman in Hamburg, Axelrath travels with her husband and becomes a close observer of Germany during the late Weimar years. She describes the gradual takeover of the Nazis from the perspective of a businessman's wife and a keen observer of the Hamburg Jewish community.

49 pp., typescript, in English, evaluation.

13. **Bach, David**; b: August 13, 1874, Vienna [d: Feb. 1, 1947, London]; Jewish; journalist and politician; last German residence: Vienna, 1940: London.

After completing his university studies with a doctorate in philosophy, the author becomes a staff writer for the Social Democratic *Arbeiterzeitung* in Vienna during 1904. Much of the memoir focuses on Bach's involvement in Social Democratic politics and culture during and after World War I. In his matter-of-fact account he tries to explain the specific social and historical circumstances of the rise of Nazism in Austria and asserts that the majority of working class Austrians remain Social Democrats at heart. The memoir does not cover events after the 1938 *Anschluss*.

22 pp., typescript.

Lit.: Röder/Strauss, NUC, GV.

14. **Baer, Ernest**

The file contains no manuscript. Correspondence indicates that the original submission, a brief essay on the psychological effects of emigration, was returned to the author.

15. **Baerwald, Alice**; b: 1883, Berlin; Jewish, m, ch:2 (sons), housewife (husband: lumber dealer); last German residence: Danzig, 1940: Cincinnati/Ohio.

The author comes from a lower-middle-class background and marries into a prosperous merchant family in 1906. The manuscript provides a lively and differentiated account of her early years in Berlin, the inter-war years, and the growth of antisemitism and Nazism in Danzig. As late as 1938, shortly before her own emigration, Baerwald is active within Zionist organizations helping Jews from Danzig to emigrate to Palestine. She leaves in 1939 via Germany, following her two sons, who are already in the United States.

80 pp., typescript, evaluation.

Lit.: Limberg/Rübsaat.

16. **Ballak, Ernst**; b: 1895, Vienna; Jewish; merchant; last German residence: Vienna, 1940: San Francisco.

The son of a wholesale merchant, the author goes to work in a military outfitter's shop at the age of sixteen and becomes the successful owner of a military supply business by World War I. He witnesses the postwar unrest in Budapest, but is back in Vienna in the early 1930s, where he observes the rise of Nazism. After the German takeover of Austria, Ballak is arrested and imprisoned in Buchenwald and Dachau concentration camps. Following his release and a short stay in Vienna, he flees via Italy, India, and Shanghai to the United States.

74 pp., typescript.

17. **Bandmann, Otto**; b: 1886; Protestant, m, ch: 2; owned news bureau; last German residence: Berlin, 1939: Amsterdam.

The file contains no manuscript; the original was returned to the author in 1947. A brief summary by one of the researchers indicates that much of the memoir deals with the author's concentration camp incarcerations in 1934 and 1938.

18. **Bartels, Elisabeth**; b: 1907, Berlin; Protestant; sales representative, travel escort, office clerk; last German residence: Berlin, 1940: London.

The illegitimate daughter of a Jewish acrobat, the author is adopted by a Christian family as a child and brought up as a Protestant. Although the authorities are not yet aware of her origins, she leaves for England in 1939 with a deep sense of alienation. Her account, which focuses on everyday life under the Nazis, deals with the conformism that governs much of German life.

19 pp., typescript, evaluation.

19. Bauer, Anton; 1940: Surrey Hills, Australia.

The main part of the manuscript is missing. Only a one-page postscript on Göring and Austrian attitudes towards Hitler remains in the file.

1 p.; handwritten.

20. "Behrendt, Hans" (pseudonym, real name: Mario Gäng); b: 1889; s; actor; last German residence: Vienna, 1940: Bronx/New York.

The lengthy memoir was returned to the author, who hoped to publish it; no such publication is known. The evaluations indicate that the manuscript contained descriptions of the author's life and arrest in Vienna and his imprisonment in Dachau concentration camp.

(14 chapters), evaluation.

Lit.: Röder/Strauss.

21. Beigel, Hugo; b. [Feb. 17] 1897, Vienna [d.: Aug 16, 1978, New York City]; Catholic, m, ch: 1; writer, psychologist; last German residence: Vienna, 1940: New York City.

The entry is organized into chapters which deal with disparate themes, not always in chronological order. The account focuses on the takeover of businesses by the Nazis and concentration camp experiences of the author's friends and colleagues.

143 pp., typescript, evaluation.

Lit.: Röder/Strauss, GV.

22. **Benk, Willy**; s; independent art historian; last German residence: Stettin, 1940: Stockholm.

From a well-to-do industrialist family, the author describes the frustration of his early ambitions to become a military officer. He takes a job as a sales representative after losing his inheritance in the inflation of the early 1920s. He joins the SA early on, but by 1931 finds himself out of favor. A conservative monarchist, he emigrates before 1934.

6 pp., typescript.

23. **Bergen, Dita**; 32, b: Southern Germany; Jewish, m; legal secretary; last German residence: Berlin, 1940: New York City.

This short memoir describes an uneventful life which is suddenly changed by the persecution of Jews after 1933.

10 pp., typescript, evaluation

24. **Berger, Moritz**; 21, b: Munich; Jewish, s; rabbinical student; last German residence: Frankfurt am Main, 1940: Brooklyn/New York.

The manuscript consists of a short story entitled "Rache" about a fourteen-year-old boy who witnesses the Nazi persecution of his family. He emigrates and dreams of returning to the land of his youth as a bomber pilot on a mission to destroy his native village.

5 pp., typescript.

25. Bernheim, Hanna; b: 1895, Southwest Germany; m, ch: 2; social worker, housewife (husband: manufacturer); last German residence: ?: 1940: Cincinnati/Ohio.

After a happy, middle-class childhood, Bernheim. marries the owner of a small-town Bavarian factory. She describes daily life in the rural town where she and her family live. The report emphasizes her family's integration into the daily life of the community despite occasional encounters with antisemitism. Only after the Nazi seizure of power (by which time they have moved to a larger town) does discrimination become overt. For the first time she takes part in the life of the Jewish community. The increasingly difficult circumstances of daily life force her to give up their business and emigrate in 1939. Largely anecdotal, this manuscript contains valuable descriptions of daily life.

66 pp., typescript, in English.

26. Berwin, Beate; Jewish; b: 1885; last German residence: ?: 1940: Cambridge/Massachusetts.

The file contains two manuscripts. One, entitled "My Own Development" by Elisabeth Morre, seems to be an autobiographical account by Berwin written under a pseudonym. It contains the story of a happy childhood and life as a literature teacher. The other part is an essay entitled "Thomas Mann's Buddenbrooks as a Source for Understanding German Psychology and Socio-Political Structure."

7 pp. ("My Own Development"); 19 pp. ("Thomas Mann"); typescript, in English.

Lit.: GV

27. Bielchowsky, Edith; b: Nov. 18, 1898; Jewish, m, ch:1; housewife (husband: lawyer), last German residence: Berlin, 1940: New York City.

The memoir is written in the guise of a novel (though the author asserts in an accompanying letter that it is autobiographical). It tells the story of a prosperous Berlin attorney and his family under the increasing pressure of the Nazis and everyday insults by antisemites. The account includes the story of the family's life in a Swiss emigré community and its residence in Monte Carlo.

57 pp., typescript.

28. **Bing, Rudolf**; 64; Jewish, m, ch:2 (daughters); lawyer; last German residence: Nuremberg, 1940: Kfar Schmaryahu/Palestine.

The memoir of this liberal Nuremberg lawyer gives a detailed account of his youth and school years. He chronicles his university studies in some detail but the story focuses on the rise of the Nazi movement in Nuremberg and its effect on the city's judicial system. The author's increasing involvement with the Zionist movement leads to his emigration to Palestine, following his daughter's earlier settlement there. The memoir also contains a dramatic account of *Kristallnacht*.

48 pp., typescript, evaluation; copy in the LBI.

29. **Bluhm, Arthur**; b: Oct. 23, 1899, Zekzin, W. Prussia; [d.: July 18, 1962, Amarillo/TX]; Jewish, m, rabbi; last German residence: Krefeld, 1940: Glencoe/Illinois.

The author gives an extensive and detailed portrait of Germany and Germans as he encountered them in his youth, during his student years in Berlin, and as a rabbi in the textile city of Krefeld. He generally describes the people he encountered in a sympathetic light. Nazis are seen as outsiders and as brutal, if effective, rulers. He is deported to Dachau concentration camp in the wake of *Kristallnacht*, but succeeds in emigrating via the Netherlands a short time later. The memoir is voluminous; it is divided into chronological and topical chapters with little continuous narrative.

232 pp., typescript, in English; microfilm negative of documents and typed translations.

Lit.: Röder/Strauss, GV. Papers: LBI.

30. **Blum, Julius**; b: 1900, near Berlin; Protestant (father: Jewish, mother: Protestant) m, ch: 1 (son); office clerk and factory worker; 1940: last German residence: ?: Cleveland/Ohio.

The short account gives the anecdotal impressions of a supporter of Social Democracy.

9 pp., typescript on microfilm, evaluation.

31. **Blumens, Siegfried**; b: Neumarkt/Poland; Jewish, m; businessman; last German residence: Berlin, 1940: Warner's Camp, Devon/ England.

The author gives a brief, anecdotal account of persons and party doctrines of the National Socialists. Correspondence indicates that he died in transit to the United States aboard the *Arandora Star*, which was sunk by German submarines in 1940.

13 pp., handwritten.

32. **Bohn, Alida**; b: 1894, New York City; m, ch: 2 (sons), housewife (husband: physicist); last German residence: Munich, 1940: Maplewood/New Jersey.

The memoir chronicles the year 1933-34, which the author spent with her family in Munich while her husband was a visiting professor of physics at the university there. While not very insightful, she records detailed impressions of everyday life.

74 pp., typescript, in English, includes photographs, clippings from *Münchner Neueste Nachrichten*, March 11, 1933.

33. "**Bollmann, Hildegard**"; 27; Protestant; university student; last German residence: Berlin, 1940: New York City.

The daughter of a conservative university professor, she grows up in modest circumstances in post-World War I Berlin. When she befriends a Jewish fellow student at the university, her brother–a Nazi–falsely accuses her of having an affair with him. She finds no backing from her family and is arrested and imprisoned. Marched through Berlin with women accused of prostitution, she is forced to confront the violence of the Nazi regime and the failure of her family to live up to its own Prussian ideals. This vivid, highly personal account also illuminates class tensions successfully exploited by the Nazis.

37 pp., typescript.

34. **Bornstein, Willy**; b: 1883, Hamburg; Jewish (wife: Protestant) m, ch: 2; petty trader; last German residence: Nuremberg; 1939: Belgium.

This brief, factual account describes personal encounters with Julius Streicher and other Nazis in Nuremberg as well as the author's flight to Brussels, where he has trouble surviving. There is no correspondence to indicate what happened to him after 1939.

13 pp., typescript, evaluation.

35. **Braasch, Elisabeth**; b: 1918, Berlin; Protestant, s; au-pair girl; last German residence: Bonn; 1940: Manhasset/New York.

This lively memoir records the impressions of a schoolgirl and young woman growing up in the 1920s and 1930s in the Rhineland. She experiences the gradual takeover of the schools by the Nazis and enters the highly regimented life of the *Arbeitsdienst*. Sent abroad to improve her English, she is unable to leave the United States after the outbreak of the war. The memoir tries to explain her contemporaries' complacency and acceptance of the Nazis.

89 pp., typescript.

36. Brehme, Claire Eichbaum; b: May 16, 1886, Berlin; Protestant, m, ch:3 (daughters); artist; 1940: Glenside/Pennsylvania.

The author submitted a book entitled "Woman of Two Countries" published by Gutenberg Press, Milwaukee. It recounts a happy youth in Germany at the turn of the century. She marries an American after World War I and emigrates with him in 1924 returning to Germany for five months in 1934. Her sympathies lie with the Nazis, whose antisemitism she shares. Although the memoir was printed by a vanity press, it was never distributed.

177 pp., book in English, evaluation. The book is in the last box of the collection.

37. Breuer, Robert; b: 1909, Vienna; journalist; last German residence: Vienna, 1940: Bronx/NY.

The manuscript contains a detailed description of the author's attempts to leave Austria for Great Britain, which are only successful after he overcomes many bureaucratic hurdles.

154 pp., typescript, on microfilm, evaluation.

Lit.: published as *Nacht über Wien: Ein Erlebnisbericht aus den Tagen des Anschlusses im März 1938* (Vienna: Löcker Verlag, 1988).

38. Breusch, Robert; b: April 2, 1907, Freiburg/Br.; Protestant, m, (wife: Jewish); mathematician; last German residence: Hinterzarten, 1940: Cambridge/Mass.

This factual account describes life in Germany during World War I and the author's university years in the Weimar Republic. The rise of antisemitism and Nazism at the university prompt him to leave academia, and he accepts a job as a mathematics teacher at a progressive boarding school. After witnessing the infiltration of Nazis into the school he decides to emigrate with his Jewish fiancé. He leaves for Chile in 1936 and enters the U.S. in 1939.

69 pp., typescript, contains partial copy of the author's detailed diary.

Lit.: Röder/Strauss, GV, NUC.

39. Broh, James; b: Nov. 9, 1867, Perleberg; Jewish, m, ch: 2; lawyer, writer, politician; last German residence: Berlin, 1940: Paris, France.

The author is brought up in a middle-class, Orthodox Jewish household. He joins the Social Democrats as a young lawyer, but in 1918 sides with the more radical USPD and becomes secretary to the executive committee of the *Räterepublik* in Berlin. Insightful and engaging, the memoir focuses on his activism in the Weimar years, during which he serves as a prominent lawyer defending socialists and Communists. He also describes the gradual change in political climate which turns friends and aquaintances into Nazis. Immediately after the Nazi seizure of power he is arrested and tortured. The circumstances of his emigration and his exile are not discussed.

148 pp., typescript.

Lit.: Röder/Strauss, GV, NUC.

40. Brüll, Paul; b: 1894, Silesia; Jewish, m, ch:2; lawyer; last German residence Krems/Austria, 1940: Jersey City/New Jersey.

The son of a sawmill operator in Austrian Silesia, the author goes to Vienna to study law before World War I. After serving in the army during the war, he continues his studies amid the disarray of political life in postwar Vienna. Brüll settles in a small town and the memoir describes the 1920s and 1930s from the perspective of a lawyer in Lower Austria. Right-wing political views and antisemitism seem to be pervasive among the author's colleagues. After the *Anschluss*, the rapid expropriation of Jews and his own arrest force him to emigrate.

82 pp., typescript, evaluation.

41. Burger, Ada; b: 1901, Berlin; s; secretary; last German residence: Berlin, 1940: Norway (?): 1943: Ecuador.

The author comes from a moderately well-to-do Berlin family. When the family loses its savings during the inflation of the early 1920s, Burger leaves high school to work as a secretary and becomes the sole support of her parents and her two younger siblings. Nevertheless she succeeds in completing her *Abitur* in night school and begins to study medicine when the Nazi seizure of power occurs. A well-known if not organized opponent of the Nazis, she is arrested in 1934 and again from 1936 to 1938. With her career and future destroyed, she leaves Germany. The memoir provides an intense and emotional, though not very cohesive, narrative.

45 pp., typescript, on microfilm, evaluation.

42. Chorin, Schalom ben; b: 1913, Munich; Jewish, m; writer, editor; last German residence: Munich, 1940: Jerusalem.

While still a student of German literature and religion, the author becomes a contributor to various Jewish and antifascist journals in Germany. The memoir describes his arrest and imprisonment in a concentration camp in great detail and with considerable literary force. He leaves Germany in 1935 to settle in Jerusalem. His literary essay describes an intellectual's passage from aestheticism to a life of political commitment.

39 pp., typescript, evaluation.

Lit.: GV.

43. Christoffers, Ella B.; b: U.S.; 1940: Norwalk/Connecticut.

The file contains only correspondence and an evaluation by the researchers. Apparently the brief manuscript was returned to the author at her request; it described her favorable impressions of Germany during her trips abroad.

44. Citron, Wolf; 35, b: [November 10. 1905] Berlin; m, Jewish; writer; last

German residence: Berlin 1940: New York City.

This concise memoir recalls a happy middle-class youth as son of a Berlin doctor. A student during the Weimar years, the author becomes aware of growing antisemitism. The report focuses on his life as a journalist and student at a time of growing Nazi domination. He gives a vivid description of the attempts of Berlin citizens to fit into the new order without disturbing old routines and friendships.

65 pp., typescript, on microfilm.

Lit.: Röder/Strauss.

45. **Czuczka, Fritz**; b: July 7, 1893, Vienna; Jewish, m, ch: 1 (son); architect; last German residence: Vienna, 1940: New York City.

The author calls himself an apolitical, middle-class Austrian. His detailed and precise report contains a description of his arrest, deportation, and imprisonment at Dachau and Buchenwald concentration camps. The report focuses on the social and psychological makeup of the SS guards and describes in detail the torture and terrorization of the prisoners as well as the everyday routines of concentration camp life.

91 pp., typescript.

46. **Daya, Werner M.**; 59; Catholic, m; head of Berlin office for iron and steel manufacturers; last German residence: Berlin, 1940: London.

Describing himself as an inventor and man of letters, the author relates his theories of Hitler's rise to power. Daya is a close observer of the Revolution of 1918-19 in Munich and author of a book on German-Russian relations which, he claims, served as a model for Hitler's policy towards Eastern Europe.

172 pp., typescript.

Lit.: NUC, GV.

47. Deutsch, Vera; b: July 10, 1895, Mährisch/Ostrau; m, ch: 1, Catholic (husband: Catholic of Jewish background); teacher (husband: economist); last German residence: Vienna, 1940: Little Rock/Arkansas.

The author gives a detailed description of her youth and schooling. After marrying her husband—an act of rebellion toward her conservative Catholic family—she becomes aware of rising antisemitism in Austria. Her husband is arrested for the first time in 1934, attempts suicide, and has to cut short flight to Czechoslovakia. The family escapes the SS and succeeds in emigrating to the U.S.

78 pp., on microfilm, typescript, evaluation.

48. Devereux, George

This file contains not a regular manuscript, but a partial copy of a letter to Dr. George Devereux, one of the evaluators, about the situation of Jews in Hungary (typed and translated into English, author unclear).

5 pp., typescript.

49. Diel, Paul; b: 1893, Vienna; Catholic, (partly Jewish ancestry), m, (wife: Jewish); writer, psychiatrist; last German residence: Vienna, 1940: Paris, later internment camp Albi/France.

This entry describes in detail the difficulties of the author, a writer of psychological studies, with Nazi-dominated publishing houses as well as the Nazi takeover of the field of psychology. Also discussed are the problems of people of partly Jewish ancestry and those in "mixed" marriages. Diel also relates the attempts of Jewish business families to survive under the Nazi regime and his own and his family's emigration to Paris.

110 pp., typescript.

Lit: NUC.

50. Dienemann, Mally; b: 1882, Gollub, Western Prussia [d.: 1963, Chicago]; Jewish, widowed, ch: 3 (daughters); housewife, (late husband: rabbi); last German residence: Offenbach/Main, 1940: Sfad/Palestine.

The daughter of a merchant from the German-Russian border, Dienemann attends school in Berlin, where she meets her future husband. She lives through World War I, the 1920s and the Nazi seizure of power as the wife of a rabbi in Upper Silesia and later near Frankfurt. After her husband's arrest and imprisonment in concentration camps, the family emigrates to Palestine in 1939. Dienemann's husband dies three weeks after their arrival.

40 pp., typescript, includes a postcard from Buchenwald, copy in the LBI.

Lit.: Limberg/Rübsaat, Richarz, vol. 2; Röder-Strauss ("Max Dienemann"). Papers of Max Dienemann: LBI.

51. Dinkel, L. M.; (originally Mayer-Dinkel, Leopold); b: January 22, 1883, Mannheim, Jewish, m, ch:1 (daughter); businessman; last German residence: Mannheim; 1940: Norwalk/Connecticut.

From a liberal Jewish family, the author recalls happy years as a schoolboy and apprentice in his father's lumber business. After military duty he travels and works abroad, operating his own business on the French-German border. He continues as a businessman in the Mannheim area after his World War I military service and watches the Weimar Republic's decay from the viewpoint of a concerned liberal. The report contains little about the period after 1933; the author begins to prepare his emigration as early as 1934 and succeeds in gaining an American visa in 1936. Throughout the report, the author maintains the viewpoint of a patriot Badener with an eye for the peculiarities of the German Southwest.

161 pp., typescript, on microfilm, includes documents.

52. Donath, Maria; 30; Catholic, m (husband: Jewish); actress; last German residence: Vienna, 1940: Great Neck/New York.

Written in a loose, anecdotal style, the narrative begins in late 1932. It relates the author's life as an actress in Berlin and other German cities and the daily humiliations and problems she and her husband face after January 1933 and is interesting for its glimpses of the theater world of Weimar Germany.

82 pp., typescript, on microfilm; file also contains an undergraduate paper analyzing the entry.

53. Drexler, Elisabeth; 45(?), b: Zittau; m, ch:1, Jewish; housewife, formerly interpreter (husband: insurance employee); last German residence: Berlin, 1940: Havana/Cuba, later: New York City.

Drexler comes from an upper-middle-class family, but has to go to work because her husband loses his job after the war. By the late 1920s both she and her husband have become professionally successful; in the early 1930s, she is a middle-class housewife. Her observations concern mostly the problems of daily life under the Nazis.

Over 120 pp. (numbered irregularly), typescript, on microfilm, evaluation.

54. Dreyfuss, Albert; 61; Jewish, m, ch: 2; physician; last German residence: Bavaria, 1940: Jerusalem.

The memoir focuses on the author's experiences as a physician with a practice in a medium-sized town in Franconia. He witnesses the rise of antisemitism in the 1920s, attacks on socialists, and the Nazi seizure of power. Dreyfuss emigrates reluctantly after nearly being deported by the Nazis. His factual and perceptive observations focus on intergenerational conflicts under the new regime and the harassment of women and children in daily life by the Nazis.

41 pp., typescript.

55. **Dudek, Erich**; b: 1905, Freiberg/Saxony; Catholic; machinist; last German residence: Chemnitz, 1939: Brussels.

Dudek is a working-class Communist who joins the political battles of the 1920s early on as a member of the Communist youth movement. His simply written, chronological account also gives details about his work experiences, arrests, incarcerations, and concentration camp experiences of 1933-1935. He emigrates via Czechoslovakia, Spain, and France to Belgium.

53 pp., handwritten, includes photographs, postcards.

56. **Elkan, Wolf**; b: 1913, Alsbach/Bergstr; Jewish; physician; last German residence: Frankfurt/Main, 1940: Jamaica Plains/Massachusetts, later: New York City.

The son of Benno Elkan, a well-known Jewish sculptor, the author grows up in small-town southern Germany aware of rising militarism and antisemitism. He begins his medical studies in Germany, but is forced to emigrate to Rome in 1934 after much harassment. After Jews are arrested in larger numbers in Rome in 1938, Elkan, by now a physician, follows his father to Great Britain and then to the United States.

121 pp., handwritten, partly typed, in English; includes news clippings.

Lit.: Limberg/Rübsaat; papers: LBI

57. **Elzholz, Paul H.**; b: Vienna; lawyer; last German residence: Vienna, 1940: Chicago.

The file contains no manuscript, but only some correspondence and an evaluation.

58. **Fabian, Alfred**; b: 1897, Berlin; Jewish, divorced; soldier, businessman; last German residence: Dresden, 1940: Shanghai.

The author, who grows up in middle-class circumstances in Berlin and

Dresden, is trained in business and film-making. As a soldier in World War I he is captured by the Russians and joins the Red Army. After fleeing the Russians and witnessing German political developments of the 1920s he is persecuted by the Nazis and put into both Dachau and Buchenwald concentration camps. Two-thirds of the manuscript contains a detailed description of life and death in Dachau and Buchenwald, 1935-1939.

303 pp., typescript, evaluation.

59. **Falkenfeld, Hellmuth**; 47, b: [1893] Fürstenwalde; Jewish, m, ch: 1(daughter); teacher, philosopher; last German residence: Berlin, 1940: New York.

The author comes from a professional family and becomes a philosophy teacher, but loses his job in 1933. An apolitical person, he is forced to emigrate after his and his wife's livelihood are destroyed by the Nazis. A considerable part of the manuscript deals with the emigration process.

51 pp., typescript, on microfilm, evaluation.

Lit.: GV, NUC.

60. **Fechenbach, Irma**; b: 1895; Jewish; w, ch: 3; nurse; 1940: St. Gallen, Switzerland: Haverford/Pennsylvania.

The file contains only correspondence, indicating that the manuscript was returned to the author at her request.

61. **Federlein, Eugene**; 42, b: Nuremberg; m; businessman; 1940: Los Angeles/California.

The author is an apolitical businessman and owner of a small factory who, after military service in World War I, succeeds in keeping his business going, largely undisturbed, until 1938. After his house is destroyed by SA members and many friends and family members are put into Dachau concentration camp, he leaves for the United States.

15 pp., typescript, on microfilm, evaluation.

62. Fiedler, Kuno; b: Feb 3, 1895, Schwiebus/Brandenburg; [d: Aug. 13, 1973, Switzerland]; Protestant, s; minister, theologian, writer; last German residence: Altenburg/Thuringia, 1940: St. Antön-ien/Switzerland.

The son of a weaver, Fiedler grows up in modest circumstances, but attends university and becomes a pastor in small-town Saxony. An article criticizing the pro-war stance of the Protestant church during World War I provokes his dismissal from the ministry in 1921. He becomes a Gymnasium teacher; dismissed from that post as well by the Nazi-dominated state government in 1932, he continues to live in Germany as a freelance contributor to Protestant newspapers. His friendship with Thomas Mann and a visit with the writer in 1936 lead to his arrest by the Gestapo and the confiscation of his property. Fiedler emigrates to Switzerland, where he becomes a pastor in a rural community.

394 pp., typescript (1/2 pages), evaluation, includes photographs and news clippings.

Lit.: Röder/Strauss; GV, NUC

63. Anonymous, c/o Fleischer, Georg (author is female); 37, b: Vienna; Jewish, m, ch: 1; lawyer, last German residence: Vienna 1940: Cambridge/Massachusetts.

The manuscript is a novella entitled "Die Geisel Gottes." According to accompanying correspondence it is autobiographical. It describes the life of an upper-class Viennese Jewish family during the years 1938/39 from a child's perspective. The detention of family members and the lengthy wait for passports and exit visas are central to the story. It was not written for the competition.

101 pp., typescript, evaluation.

64. Flesch, Philipp; b: 1896, Vienna; s. Jewish; teacher, last German residence: Vienna, 1940: New York City.

The author describes his youth and World War I army service as relatively uneventful. He takes up language study at the University of Vienna and becomes a teacher at a *Realgymnasium*, a position he holds until 1938. Confronted with antisemitism and what he sees as the breakdown of Austrian society after 1938, he leaves in 1939.

41 pp., typescript, on microfilm, evaluation; original at the LBI.

65. "Flynn, Lilian" (pseudonym); b: 1895, Vienna; Catholic, divorced, ch: 1 (son); photographer; last German residence: Berlin, 1940: New York City.

An independent news photographer in Berlin, the author recalls her happy and prosperous childhood in Vienna and her brief film career as a young woman. The loosely structured memoir gives a series of sketchy impressions of life from the Austro-Hungarian Empire years of her childhood to her adult years in Nazi Berlin.

68 pp., typescript.

66. Frank, Ernest; 45, b: 1895, Cologne; Jewish, m, ch: 1 (son); author, stage manager, actor; last German residence: Berlin, 1940: New York City.

From an upper-class Cologne family, the author recalls his experiences with conservative nationalist teachers as a schoolboy, his army service in World War I and his encounters with National Socialists during the early 1920s. The memoir is loosely structured and anecdotal.

112 pp., typescript, evaluation.

67. Frankenthal, Käthe; b: Jan. 30, 1889, Kiel; [d: April 21, 1976, New

York]; Jewish; physician; last German residence: Berlin; 1940: New York City.

A physician and socialist activist, the author perceptively sketches her girlhood in a comfortable bourgeois family. Most of this precise and literary memoir is devoted to her years as a physician in working-class districts and as a socialist politician in Berlin during the 1920s.

317 pp., typescript, 20-dollar prizewinner.

Lit.: The manuscript was published as *Der dreifache Fluch: Jüdin, Intellektuelle, Sozialistin Lebenserinnerungen einer Ärztin in Deutschland und im Exil*, ed. Kathleen Pearle and Stephan Leibfried (Frankfurt: Campus, 1981); Röder/Strauss; GV, NUC.

68. **Freudenheim, Martin**; b: 1875, Berlin; Jewish, m; lawyer; last German residence: Berlin, 1940: Tel Aviv.

The author describes his youth in Berlin as the son of Jews from Posen. The influence of antisemitic movements is evident during his school years. The author's impressions of Germans as subservient to authority are confirmed when he serves as an officer during World War I. The war years also reinforce Freudenheim's Social Democratic convictions. The memoir also contains observations on the position of Jewish lawyers in the judicial system and on the Revolution of 1918/19.

80 pp., typescript, evaluation.

69. **Friedländer, Karl**; b: April 9, 1882, Pless/Oberschlesien; Jewish, m; lawyer; last German residence: Berlin, 1940: Chicago/Illinois.

After an education in Jewish elementary schools and a secular Gymnasium, the author studies law and becomes a lawyer in Berlin, but assumes the position of legal counsel to an industrial concern in 1919. Labor negotiations are the focus of his activity, and the memoir contains valuable insights into the relationship between heavy industry and the Nazis. Friedländer also describes the difficulties of emigration.

86 pp., typescript, evaluation.

Lit.: Limberg/Rübsaat.

70. **Friedwald, Adolph**; b: 1895, Polish Russia; Jewish; 1940: New York City.

The author is an American who spent the World War I years in Germany. The first part of the manuscript contains a memoir of those years, the second part a description and refutation of Nazi propaganda.

22 pp., handwritten in English, on microfilm; evaluation; original returned to the author.

71. **Ganser, Harald** (pseudonym: "Timon Expulsus"); b: 1902; Protestant; teacher; last German residence: Central German City of 100,000: 1940: Pasadena.

In his short report, the author describes his expulsion from academia and his internment in Dachau as a member of the *Bekennende Kirche*.

7 pp., typescript, in English.

72. **Gebhard, Bruno**; b: Feb. 1, 1901, Rostock; Protestant, m, ch: 3 (daughters); physician, museum curator; last German residence: Berlin, 1939: Manhasset/Long Island.

A conservative Prussian, the author describes his student years and his political involvement with anti-revolutionary forces after World War I. He becomes a museum curator at the Dresden Museum for Public Health and later assumes a similar position in Berlin, where he is at first supportive of the National Socialists and continues to organize public health exhibits. But his attempts to conform with the new regime as a professional and German nationalist run into trouble after 1934. A trip to the U.S. confronts him with the problem of reconciling the "real" Germany as he comes to see it from afar with Nazi propaganda. He decides to stay in the United States during a second professional visit in 1937.

105 pp., typescript, in English.

Lit.: Röder/Strauss; GV, NUC.

73. **Geffner, Max**; b: 1904, Western Ukraine/Austria; Jewish; teacher for the blind; last German residence: Vienna, 1940: New York City.

This memoir focuses on the author's activism on behalf of the blind. Geffner grows up in a small town in the western Ukraine and as a result of an accident becomes completely blind by age 14; he enters a school for the blind in Vienna, where he is dissatisfied with the manual skills taught to him. After entering university in the 1920s he overcomes considerable difficulties and finishes with a doctorate in German literature. A lecturer and book collector, he becomes active as a collector of Braille books and as a Social Democrat in the early 1930s. After the *Anschluss* he is able to emigrate via Great Britain to the US in 1939/1940.

94 pp., typescript, on microfilm, evaluation.

Lit.: GV.

74. **Geisler, Marianne**; 48, Catholic (formerly Protestant, husband Jewish), m, ch: 2 (son, daughter); physician, last German residence, Ratibor, 1940: Galion/Ohio.

This memoir tells the story of a highly emotional and sensitive woman who, after a lower-middle-class childhood in Danzig, studies medicine and settles with her first husband in small-town Mecklenburg. She becomes a Social Democrat, but is not politically active during the Weimar years. After the death of her first husband, she and her fiancé emigrate to Central China, where they are married. After practicing medicine in China they return to Germany in 1934 and settle in Upper Silesia. Since her second husband is Jewish, they soon try to emigrate again and eventually secure an American visa.

51 pp., typescript, on microfilm, evaluation.

75. Glas, Emil; 60, b: Vienna; Protestant (Jewish descent), m; professor of medicine; 1940: New York City.

In this loosely structured memoir, the author reminisces about his childhood and professional life; he also records incidents in his and his friends' life under Nazi rule in Austria.

84 pp., handwritten, on microfilm (faded), evaluation.

76. Glaser, Julius; b: 1882, Travemünde; Jewish, m, ch: 1 (daughter); upholsterer; last German residence: Cologne, Leipzig, 1939: Nice, 1941: Gurs/France.

In this brief, factual memoir, the author describes his persecution and flight. A skilled worker and active Communist, he receives support from neighbors and friends while still in Germany.

12 pp., handwritten, includes photo.

77. Goetz, Fritz; [b. 1876, Breslau, journalist editor.] 1940: Tel Aviv.

The file is empty.

Papers: LBI.

78. Goldman, Leopold

This file contains correspondence and a poem entitled "Vogelballade"; the poem contains no biographical information, and none is available in the file.

7 pp., handwritten.

79. Goldschmidt, Fritz; 46, b: Breslau, [d: London 1968]; Jewish, m, ch:2; judge; last German residence: Berlin, 1940: London.

This file contains only correspondence and an evaluation by the researchers. The manuscript was returned to the author at his request. According to the evaluation, the author comes from an assimilated Jewish family and enters a legal career, but is prevented from becoming a university teacher because of his refusal to convert to Christianity. Instead he becomes a judge and an active member of the "Centralverein deutscher Staatsbürger jüdischen Glaubens." Dismissed in 1933, he works for the Centralverein full-time until his arrest in 1938 and a two-week imprisonment in Sachsenhausen concentration camp. [Goldschmidt emigrated to London in 1939.]

No manuscript, evaluation only. Original in the LBI.

Lit.: Röder/Strauss.

80. **Goldstein, Arthur**; b: 1899, Bukovina; Jewish, s; lumber dealer; last German residence: Vienna, 1940: Shanghai.

This short memoir reports on the author's youth in Bukovina, his experiences as a successful businessman during the 1920s and the antisemitism of the 1930s. It also describes his emigration to Shanghai and his efforts to survive there.

9 pp., typescript.

81. **Gottheil, Walter**; b: 1883; Jewish, m, ch: 1 (son); businessman; last German residence: Berlin, 1940: Tel Aviv.

Gottheil describes a childhood marred by antisemitism and Christian proselytizing efforts. He becomes a Zionist early on and is active in Jewish organizations until his arrest in 1938. He is freed after receiving a visa for Palestine. The bitter tone of this memoir also reflects his painful coming to terms with his Jewish identity.

66 pp., typescript, last page handwritten, evaluation.

82. Gottlieb, Max; Jewish.

This memoir contains a detailed description of the author's incarceration in Sachsenhausen concentration camp. It was not part of the original collection, but was sent to the researchers by Charles Sass of Philadelphia at a later date. No biographical data on the author are available.

36 pp., typescript, in English.

83. Gottschalk, Friedrich; b: 1868, Bernburg; Jewish, m, ch.: 2 (son and daughter); lawyer; last German residence: Bernburg, 1940: Haifa/Palestine.

The author lives in his native town until his emigration in 1934, with some interruptions during World War I and his student years. His memoir describes in perceptive detail the texture of small-town life for German Jews, mainly before 1914. It also contains lively portraits of university life before World War I and a description of the author's war service and legal practice during the 1920s and 1930s.

Over 297 pp., typescript, incomplete, final pages missing.

84. Grünebaum, Leo; b: 1888, Wenings/Oberhessen; Jewish, m, ch: 2 (son and daughter); teacher, administrator; last German residence: Cologne, 1940: Bridgeport/Connecticut.

An observant Jew from a village in Hesse, the author describes his life in rural Germany around the turn of the century. After university studies and military service in World War I, Grünebaum begins a career as a Jewish educator and administrator in Cologne. The memoir also describes the life of his family and friends under Nazi rule in Cologne and rural Hesse.

43 pp., typescript, evaluation, includes original documents.

Lit.: Limberg/Rübsaat.

85. Günzberger, Siegmund; b: 1882; Jewish, m, ch: 3; businessman, owner of cabaret; last German residence: Berlin, 1940: Stockholm/Sweden.

This short memoir focuses on the author's war adventures as a prisoner in Russia during World War I, his bankruptcy in 1932, and his difficulties emigrating and surviving as a businessman in Sweden.

9 pp., typescript, includes original documents.

86. Gyssling, Walter; b: [March 18] 1903, Munich, d: [1980]; Protestant, divorced, ch: 1 (daughter); journalist; last German residence: Berlin, 1939: Paris, 1940: Zurich.

The author grows up in a wealthy home but becomes a left-wing journalist after his university years. As an editor for the *Süddeutsche Zeitung*, he witnesses the growth of Nazism and decides to leave for Switzerland in March, 1933. His lively memoir combines personal memories of the 1920s and 1930s with general observations on Germany's political and social condition.

103 pp., typescript, awarded third prize of $100.

Lit.: A published edition of the manuscript, edited by Leonidas E. Hill and with an introduction by Arnold Paucker, is forthcoming (Bremen, Donat Verlag). Röder/Strauss, GV, NUC; Leonidas E. Hill, "Walter Gyssling, the Centralverein and the Büro Wilhelmstrasse, 1929-1933," *Leo Baeck Institute Yearbook* 38 (1993), 193-208; papers: LBI.

87. Hallgarten, Constance; m, ch: 1 (son); feminist/pacifist activist (husband: literature scholar); last German residence: Munich, 1940: Palo Alto/California.

As the wife of a wealthy independent scholar of German literature, the author moves in upper-class circles beginning in the early twentieth century. After a happy and sheltered childhood she gets involved in volunteer activities during World War I. Her political activism begins in 1914 and leads her to direct the World Peace League (*Weltfriedensbund*). She describes in detail her involvement in numerous pacifist and feminist organizations before and after World War I and her acquaintances with many well-known personalities of the Weimar era. The memoir contains very little on the 1930s.

102 pp., typescript, bound.

Lit.: GV, NUC.

88. **Harpuder, Erich** (pseud.: "Erich Drucker").

The file contains no manuscript or evaluation; correspondence indicates that the file was sent to Hartshorne in March 1942.

89. **"Hay, John"** (pseudonym); 41, b: Stettin; Jewish, m, ch: 2; actor, journalist, teacher; last German residence: Berlin, 1940: New York City.

The author describes his childhood in Alsace and sheds light on the relations between Jews, French, and Germans there before World War I. After the war he moves to Berlin and becomes active in the theater. The memoir focuses on the role of Jews in the theater world and their vulnerability to Nazi attacks, especially after 1933. The author also writes about the birth of his children in 1937 and 1938, his experiences during *Kristallnacht* and his internment in an unnamed concentration camp.

62 pp., typescript.

90. **Haynes, Edna M.**; 40, b: Bayside/Long Island; m, ch: 2 (sons); housewife, (husband: jockey, horse trainer, businessman); last German residence: Berlin, 1933: Oklahoma City/Oklahoma.

The author, an American, lived in Berlin from 1925 to mid-1933, when her husband was a jockey and horse trainer on the Berlin race track. She describes the sporting life of the 1920s and the beginnings of antisemitism and persecution of Jews from the perspective of an American outraged by the growing police state.

53 pp., typescript, includes news clippings, photographs.

91. **Hecht, Carl**; 48, b: Metz; Jewish, s; bank clerk, last German residence: Frankfurt am Main, 1940: New York City.

The short memoir contains a description of the author's arrest during *Kristallnacht*, his deportation to and imprisonment in Buchenwald, and his flight from Germany.

15 pp., typescript.

92. **Heilpern, Edmund**; b: 1892; Jewish; in advertising; last German residence: Vienna, 1940: Topeka/Kansas.

The author relates his experiences during World War I and as an advertising man during the 1920s. His observations are impressionistic and touch on topics including his involvement with Anthroposophy and Spiritism, Jewish life in Vienna, the opposition of proletarian and avant-garde culture, and the author's own experience and imprisonment under Nazi rule. The memoir is not organized chronologically.

142 pp., typescript, evaluation; prizewinner (amount not stated).

93. **Hellwig, Verena**; b: 1897, Southwest Germany; Protestant, widowed (husband: "half-Jewish"); housewife, formerly teacher (late husband: insurance executive); last German residence: Baden, 1940: Newlands/South Africa.

This factual memoir tells the story of an upper-middle-class woman's experiences during World War I and the 1920s and the increasing rejection of her as the wife of a "*Mischling*" during the 1930s. Much of the memoir deals with the family's emigration to South Africa, which takes much preparation and stretches over almost two years. Her husband is the last to emigrate. He commits suicide in the fall of 1939, shortly after the family's arrival in Africa.

66 pp., typescript, evaluation.

94. "Hempel" (pseudonym); b: 1917; Jewish, m; picture frame maker; last German residence: Berlin, 1940: Switzerland.

A Jewish socialist with some higher education, H. flees to France in 1933. He returns to Germany in 1935 and works there until 1937; in 1938 he flees again, this time to Switzerland. The memoir captures the mood of a socialist with a very critical, anti-bourgeois perspective, whose rejection of German society is deeply personal rather than politically motivated.

26 pp., typescript.

95. Herrmann, Ludwig; Jewish; 1939: Johannesburg, South Africa.

This short report contains no biographical information, but instead describes three incidents through which the author experienced the transformation of German society after the Nazi seizure of power.

3 pp., handwritten.

96. Herz, Sofoni; 34, b: Heppenheim (?); Jewish, s; journalist, educator; last German residence: Cologne, 1940: Sydney/Australia, internment camp.

From an Orthodox Jewish home, the author describes his development into a socialist and journalist. During the early 1920s and again after 1933 H. works as teacher in orphanages and other institutions for Jewish children. The last part of the memoir contains a detailed, factual description of his experience of *Kristallnacht* in the Jewish orphanage which he headed in 1938.

39 pp., typescript, includes photographs.

97. **Hirschberg, Max**; 56, b: 1883, Munich [d: 1964, USA]; Jewish, m, ch: 1 (son); lawyer; last German residence: Munich, 1939: New York City.

The son of a Munich merchant, the author describes his encounters with antisemitism and the judicial system before and after World War I. He becomes a prominent lawyer and one of the defense attorneys in the *Dolchstossprozesse*, which are described in detail in the memoir. His astute observations focus on the judicial system and reach up to 1934, when he leaves Germany.

102 pp., typescript, evaluation.

Lit.: Max Hirschberg, *Jude und Demokrat: Erinnerungen eines Münchner Rechtsanwalts, 1883-1939*, ed. Reinhard Weber (Munich: Oldenbourg, 1998).

Lit.: NUC, GV. Papers: LBI.

98. **Ibsen, Henry**, 1940: New York.

The short manuscript consists of excerpts from letters which his mother wrote to him about her deportation from Germany to Poland in 1939. It contains no biographical data on the author.

3 pp., typescript.

99. **Jahndorf, Ernst**.

The file contains no memoir; apparently the researchers sent the manuscript back but kept an excerpt entitled "Letter from Ernst to Georg," dated March 30, 1939. It describes a trip to Dachau in 1938.

5 pp., typescript.

100. **Jaraz, Stephen W.** (pseudonym: "Reginald Ray"); b: 1906, Vienna; Protestant (father: Jewish), m; lawyer; last German residence: Vienna, 1940: Gosford/Australia.

The son of a middle-class, assimilated Jewish family, Jaraz describes his years as a boy and as a student in post-World War I Vienna. From the viewpoint of a young lawyer, he pays special attention to the changes in the judicial system and the intricacies of Austrian domestic politics during the 1930s. He witnesses the massive brutality against Jews and critics of the system after the Austrian *Anschluss*. He himself is taken prisoner, questioned by the Gestapo, and then deported to Dachau and Buchenwald. This factual and very perceptive report provides a close and powerful description of the concentration camps and their inmates.

108 pp., typescript, evaluation.

101. **Kahle, Maria**; b: May 6, 1893, Berlin [d: 1948, England]; Catholic (formerly: Protestant), m, ch: 5 (sons); elementary school teacher, housewife, (husband: university professor); last German residence: Bonn, 1940: Kew, Surrey/England.

The wife of a prominent university professor, Kahle describes the Nazi takeover in her hometown from the perspective of a previously apolitical housewife and mother. Her short, factual and perceptive report focuses on the effects of the Hitler youth movement on children and families. After she and her sons try to help Jewish neighbors in the wake of *Kristallnacht*, they are publicly denounced in the local newspaper. Her husband loses his professorship and she is put under virtual house arrest. With some difficulty, the family flees to England in the spring of 1939.

15 pp., typescript.

Lit.: NUC, Röder/Strauss ("Paul Kahle").

102. **Kalisher, Marianne**; b: 1895, Vienna; Jewish, m; administrative assistant, (husband: lawyer); last German residence: Vienna, 1940:

Portland/Oregon.

The author describes her upbringing in a middle-class Viennese Jewish family. Her report focuses on the relations between Jews and non-Jews in Austria before and after World War I. She experiences the post-World War I period as a time of great uncertainty. The Nazi takeover of Austria prompts her family's emigration to the United States via France. The process leading to emigration is described in some detail.

56 p., typescript, evaluation.

103. **Kamm, Berta S.**; 50, b: eastern provinces of Germany; Jewish, m, ch: 2 (son and daughter); high school teacher (husband: lawyer); last German residence: Breslau, 1940: Berkeley/California.

The author describes her late start in higher education at the age of forty in 1930. She enters university to study law until 1933; she and her family leave Germany in the spring of that year. The report follows the family's emigration to Paris via Switzerland and finally to the United States in 1936.

80 pp., typescript, on microfilm, evaluation, includes documents.

104. **Kastan, Benno**; b: 1896, Prenzlau; Jewish; physician; last German residence: Berlin, 1940: Long Island City/NY.

The short report describes the author's years as a family physician in Berlin, his persecution as a Jew during the Nazi years, and his imprisonment in Sachsenhausen concentration camp in 1938.

7 pp., typescript, evaluation.

Lit.: GV.

105. **Kastan, Dr. Max**; 55; Jewish, m; physician, professor at medical school, psychiatrist; last German residence: Königsberg, 1940: Cincinnati/Ohio.

The author describes his youth as a member of a traditional Jewish family in Berlin and his Gymnasium education. The account also focuses on his medical school education, his experiences as a physician at the University of Heidelberg before and after World War I, and his persecution after 1933.

23 pp., handwritten, difficult to read.

106. **Katz, H. W.**; 32; Jewish, m, ch; journalist, editor; 1940: Brooklyn/NY.

The file contains no manuscript. Correspondence indicates that the author submitted a novel, which the researchers encouraged him to send to Viking Press. Viking published it under the title *No. 21 Castle St.*

Evaluation.

Lit.: Manuscript was published as: *No 21 Castle Street*, trans. Norbert Guterman, (New York, 1940). German: H.W. Katz, *Schlossgasse 21: In einer kleinen deutschen Stadt* (Weinheim: Beltz Quadriga, 1994).

Lit.: GV, NUC.

107. **Kaufman, Hans**; b: 1911, Dortmund; Jewish; owner of a shoe store; last German residence: Essen, 1940: Dover/New Hampshire.

The brief entry contains general observations on the nature of life under National Socialism by a conservative. The manuscript emphasizes the presence of widespread inner resistance to the regime.

12 pp., typescript, in English, evaluation.

108. **Kaufman, Harry**; 27; Jewish, m; manager in shoe business; last German residence: Essen, 1940: Dover/New Hampshire.

The author witnesses the occupation of the Rhineland by French troops during his youth and adds observations on social conditions in Weimar Germany. The memoir also contains general descriptions of daily life under the Nazis. It stresses the loss of individual freedom and the persecution of Jews. As a nationalist Jew the author offers a cautious assessment of the regime.

70 pp., typescript, evaluation; biographical details resemble those of Hans Kaufman's entry, but style and emphasis as well as length of the two memoirs differ greatly.

109. Kekone, Pauline; 70, b: Raschwitz/Upper Silesia; Baptist; 1940: Milwaukee/Wisconsin.

This brief memoir by a German immigrant woman who settled in Milwaukee in 1891 contains no references to the 1930s. It concerns mainly her childhood in rural Silesia and emigration as a young woman to the United States.

21 pp., handwritten.

110. Kessel, Susan and Kessel, Christine; b: 1870 and 1874; Christian Scientists, s; retail clerks; 1940: Newark/New Jersey.

The authors are Americans of German parentage who describe their first visit to Germany in 1937. Recounting their trip through Berlin and various Rheinland cities, the authors assert that Hitler has brought peace to Germany. The manuscript has strong antisemitic undertones.

16 pp., typescript.

111. Kirschnek, Jean; b: 1902, Selb/Bayern; Protestant; worker; last German residence: Hof, 1940: Warwick/England.

The working-class author begins his brief memoir with a short description of his years as a soldier in World War I and the 1920s in the town of Selb. As socialists, both the author and his brother are imprisoned in 1933. The author's brother dies in Dachau; he himself is deported to Czechoslovakia and flees from there to France in 1939.

21 pp., typescript, on microfilm, evaluation.

112. Klein, Hans C.; 1940: Brooklyn/New York.

The file contains only correspondence indicating that the manuscript was returned to the author.

113. Klugmann, Dr. Hermann; b: 1885, Wiesenbronn/Unterfranken; Jewish, m, ch: 1 (son); high school teacher; last German residence: Munich, 1940: Allston/Massachusetts.

This detached chronological memoir by a conservative teacher focuses on the effects of National Socialism and antisemitism on school life and the education system. The author remembers his own youth in rural Germany and his relations to non-Jewish school children in this setting. The characterizations of emerging Nazi influence in his hometown and on the public schools are precise and specific. He also describes his flight to the United States via Switzerland and the help he gets from sympathetic friends in Germany.

81 pp., typescript, evaluation.

Lit.: Limberg/Rübsaat.

114. Koch, F.; 49, b: Dresden; m (wife: Hilde Koch, entry 115); toolmaker; last German residence: Berlin, 1940: East Orange/New Jersey.

A revolutionary worker, the author begins his memoir with a description of his days as a soldier from 1911 to the end of World War I, an experience which turns him into an anti-militarist. It also matter-of-factly and briefly relates his life history during the years of postwar revolution, economic crisis, and inflation during the 1920s; he views the Nazi seizure of power in the context of mass unemployment. Engaging in illegal political activism in 1933, the author is arrested and incarcerated in Sonnenburg concentration camp. After his release he flees to the U.S. via Switzerland.

109 pp., typescript, evaluation.

115. **Koch, Hilde**; 34, b: Dresden; Protestant, m (husband: F. Koch, entry 114); bookkeeper; last German residence: Berlin; 1940: East Orange/New Jersey.

The author's report focuses on themes different from her husband's: domestic and family life during World War I and the 1920s and 1930s. She maintains the perspective of a class-conscious socialist in her memoir, which focuses on the lengthy and anxious time of waiting after her husband's arrest by the SA. She also describes at length the emigration process and her arrival in the United States.

151 pp., typescript, evaluation.

Lit.: Parts of the story were published anonymously and in somewhat altered form in *Refugee*, trans. Clara Leiser (New York: Prentice-Hall, 1940).

116. **Koganowsky, Maximilian Georg**; 37, b: 1903; Catholic, m; newspaper editor; last German residence: Vienna, 1940: New York City.

The author, formerly a journalist for the *Reichspost*, a Catholic paper, describes Austrian politics during the 1920s and 1930s. After the *Anschluss* he is arrested and deported to Dachau, where he is tortured by the SS. The report focuses on his experiences in Dachau, the daily routines and cruelties of the concentration camps, and his eventual release.

175 pp., typescript, on microfilm, evaluation. The original was returned to the author, who indicated his desire to publish it. No publication is known.

117. **Kollander, David**; 31; Jewish, s; lumber salesman and physical education teacher; last German residence: Leipzig, 1940: New York City.

The loosely structured, impressionistic memoir begins with the author's arrival in the United States in 1935 but focuses on his experiences as a Zionist youth in Germany during the 1920s. Antisemitism in the schools and postwar economic problems are also important themes in this manuscript

49 pp., typescript.

118. **Kosterlitz, Hans**; 34, b: 1906, Breslau; Jewish, m; manager of retail store; last German residence: Berlin, 1940: Shanghai.

The manuscript gives a chronological account of the author's experiences as an active supporter of Weimar democracy, an apprentice during the 1920s, and a manager of a retail store that was put under boycott by the Nazis. The memoir also describes the disintegration of his love affair with a non-Jewish woman under the pressure of small-town Nazi antisemitism.

36 pp., typescript, evaluation.

Lit.: Limberg/Rübsaat.

119. **Kranzler, Georg**; 24, b: Würzburg; Jewish, s; university student, office clerk; last German residence: Berlin, 1940: Brooklyn/New York.

The brief manuscript describes the deterioration of a friendship with a non-Jewish woman after the Nazi seizure of power.

5 pp., typescript.

120. **Kretschmar, Julius**; b: 1892, Breslau; Jewish, m, ch: 1 (daughter); physician; last German residence: Emden/Ostfriesland, 1940: Ra'ananna/Palestine.

The son of a middle-class family of patriotic German Jews, the author describes his youth in Breslau and his years as a young doctor in Pomerania, where he meets members of the Polish intelligentsia. During World War I and until his emigration he practices as an internist in East Friesland where he raises a family in the 1920s and is exposed to Nazi terror tactics after 1933. Active in Zionist organizations from the 1920s on, he makes a preliminary trip to Palestine in the early 1930s, but does not settle there until after his arrest and concentration camp incarceration in 1938.

83 pp., typescript, evaluation.

121. **Krichtensen, Hermann**; b: 1891; m, ch: 1 (son); businessman; 1940: London.

This brief account describes the author's imprisonment in Buchenwald in 1938 and his subsequent release in 1939. He leaves for Cuba on the *St. Louis*, but since the ship is denied permission to dock in Cuba, he instead ends up in London.

4 pp., handwritten.

122. **Kromayer, Heinrich**; b: Oct. 29, 1900, Freiberg/Saxony; Protestant, m (wife: Jewish), ch: 2; teacher; last German residence: Berlin, 1940: East Orange/New Jersey.

From a middle-class family of pastors and teachers, the author focuses his memoir on his experiences as a Social Democratic teacher in the vocational education system of the Weimar Republic. Removed from his teaching post before 1933 by the Nazi-dominated state authorities in Thuringia, he moves to other parts of the country, continuing his work in vocational education schools until he is forced to emigrate. The memoir contains analytical reflections on the progress of and support for National Socialism in Thuringia.

66 pp., typescript, evaluation.

123. **Kronenberg, Max** (pseudonym: "Clemens Berg"); 46; Jewish, m, ch: 1 (daughter); engineer; last German residence: Berlin, 1940: Cincinnati/Ohio.

This brief manuscript describes the author's middle-class background, his experiences during World War I, and his professional activities as an engineer and teacher at the Technical University of Berlin. The manuscript also deals with his gradual realization that his personal freedom is unbearably limited after 1933, which leads to his and his family's emigration.

24 pp., typescript, evaluation.

Lit.: GV.

124. **Krug, Lily**; 43; Jewish, w; journalist; last German residence: Hamburg, 1940: San Francisco/California.

This memoir contains very little information on the years before 1933. Certain parts focus on the persecution of Jews after 1933. The author describes in detail her brother's incarceration in Sachsenhausen concentration camp. Intermingled are descriptions of her adventures in different parts of the world after her emigration as well as her observations on the effects of Hitler in Germany. The narrative is highly disjointed, and the descriptions are anecdotal.

69 pp., typescript, in English.

125. **Kurz, Emil**; 40, Jewish; s, lawyer; last German residence: Vienna, 1940: Minneapolis/Minnesota.

Entitled "Das Märtyrium der Juden in Österreich," the manuscript describes the persecution of Jews in Austria during the summer of 1938, deportations, and torture in considerable detail. It contains no biographical information and was completed in the fall of 1938, before announcement of the essay contest was made.

35 pp., typescript.

126. **Landau, Edwin**; b: 1890, Deutsch-Krone/West Prussia [d. 1975, Israel];

Jewish, m, ch: 2 (sons); owner of hardware store, plumber; last German residence: Deutsch-Krone, 1940: Ramat-Gan/Palestine.

The author recounts his youth in a small town as the son of the local hardware store owner. He becomes active in Jewish youth groups and moves to Berlin as a young man but returns to his hometown to take over his father's business. The memoir describes his conversion to Zionism as a middle-aged man who, despite his deep roots in the Jewish community of his home country, leaves Germany as early as 1934 to settle in Palestine. He ultimately views this as a positive decision. The manuscript includes excerpts from the author's diary as a soldier and a number of poems written before 1933.

52 pp., typescript.

Lit.: Limberg/Rübsaat, Richarz, vol. 3. Papers: LBI.

127. **Lange, Helen**; b: 1898, Russia; Jewish, m; last German residence: Berlin, 1940: New York City.

This lengthy memoir begins with a description of the author's happy childhood in a politically progressive, Russian Jewish family in St.Petersburg. Having finished her university studies, she marries a German and moves to Germany in 1926. After divorcing him she marries the writer Peter Lange and becomes an active speaker and writer for progressive republican causes in the later years of the Weimar Republic. Well known as an anti-Nazi, her husband is arrested almost immediately after the Nazi seizure of power and put into a concentration camp. With the help of friends, the couple secures emigration visas to London in 1934.

260 pp., typescript, on microfilm, (partly illegible), in English, evaluation.

128. **Laué, Ruth Heidi**; b: 1914, Danzig; Protestant, s; secretary; last German residence: Hamburg, 1939: Hamburg.

This detailed memoir by a young German (who spent two years in the

United States as a college student) recounts her childhood as a German in Danzig and her impressions of the supposed dangers posed by Communism and Jews in the Weimar years. The account gradually discloses her conviction that National Socialism has provided the best solution to Germany's and that Hitler's regime is misleadingly portrayed in the American press.

65 pp., typescript.

129. **Lawrence, Robert E.**; 29, b: Vienna; Jewish, m; lawyer; last German residence: Vienna, 1940: Albany/New York.

From a middle-class, professional family, the author describes his experiences with antisemitism as a schoolboy and at the university as well as in a factory where he works part-time to earn money. After a cursory account of political developments during the early and mid-1930s in Austria, especially at the University of Vienna, he focuses in detail on the events accompanying the *Anschluss* in 1938. While waiting for a visa to the United States, he witnesses the terrorism and systematic stripping away of property and livelihood of Austrian Jews.

55 pp., typescript, evaluation.

130. **Lederer, Gertrude Wickerhauser**; 43, b: 1897, Vienna; Catholic, (husband: Jewish), m, ch: 3; translator, writer (husband: physician); last German residence: Vienna, 1940: Wilmington/Delaware.

A liberal, the author describes her life in Vienna's professional middle class from her own, not very political perspective, and she also includes the viewpoints of other members of her family. The account focuses on the years 1938-39, which are recounted in great detail. Her husband's arrest and her own efforts to get visas to emigrate for herself and her family are the central events in this engagingly written memoir.

230 pp., typescript.

Lit.: GV.

131. Lehmann, Otto (pseudonym: "Borner, X.Y."); b: 1873, Berlin; Protestant, w, ch: 3; writer, book dealer; last German residence: Berlin, 1940: London.

The author is born into a chaotic family of lower-middle-class postal workers. He becomes a confirmed pacifist and atheist early on and sees himself to be in perpetual conflict with the Protestant church and society at large. A polemicist against Germany's armaments industry, he is arrested as early as 1933 and emigrates to the Netherlands in the same year. From there he flees to England. While neither cohesive nor analytical, the memoir contains interesting insights into the world of pacifists and nonconformists.

127 pp., typescript, evaluation.

132. Leichtentritt, Hugo; b: Jan 1, 1874, Posen [d: Nov 13, 1951, Cambridge/Massachusetts]; music teacher and critic.

The file contains no manuscript, but only correspondence indicating that the manuscript was returned to the author. A brief summary describes it as long and devoted primarily to musical life and musicians, subjects that were not of interest to the evaluators.

In English.

Lit.: Röder/Strauss. Papers: University of Utah, Library of Congress, LBI.

133. Lessler, Toni (Mrs.) [b: Bückeburg, 1874, social worker, teacher; last German residence: Berlin] 1940: New York.

The file contains no manuscript or evaluation; correspondence indicates that it was returned to the author in 1950.

Manuscript original in the LBI.

134. Levi, Julius Walter; [b. Oct. 9, 1891 in Munich, physician]; writer, humorist; 1940: New York City.

The file contains only correspondence and an evaluation.

The evaluation states that it was the most humorous entry. The manuscript was returned to the author in 1961 at his request.

Manuscript original at the LBI.

Lit.: NUC. Papers: LBI.

135. Levy, Joseph B; 69, b: Kiel [d: 1966, New York City]; Jewish, m, ch: 4; teacher, cantor; last German residence: Frankfurt am Main, 1940: Dorchester/Massachusetts.

From a family of rabbis, the author becomes a teacher in Jewish schools of Wilhelmine Germany. A well-integrated German nationalist, active in the Centralverein deutscher Staatsbürger jüdischen Glaubens, he describes the rise of antisemitism in the schools during the 1930s and the founding of separate Jewish schools by the Jews of Frankfurt. His generally positive feelings about Germany are tested (though not wholly destroyed) by his arrest, *Kristallnacht*, and his struggle to emigrate.

90 pp., typescript, includes documents also on microfilm, copy in the LBI; received a $20.00 prize.

Lit.: Limberg/Rübsaat.

136. Levy, Leopold; 66; Jewish; grocer; last German residence: Berlin, 1940: Philadelphia/Pennsylvania.

The manuscript contains a brief report on the life of a small grocery owner in Berlin during the 1930s.

3 pp., typescript, evaluation.

137. **Lewinsohn, Martha**; 39; m, ch: 1 (son); housewife, (husband: electrician); last German residence: Dresden, 1939: Copenhagen, 1940: Visby/Sweden.

This brief, perceptive account describes a working-class family's efforts to escape Nazi persecution. Since both the author and her husband are Communists, this involves destruction of a library and files. She experiences both support and denunciations by neighbors. After her husband's incarceration, he is freed with the help of Quaker organizations. He emigrates to Denmark in 1937.

7 pp., typescript, evaluation.

138. **Lichtenstein, Heinrich F.**; b: Dec. 15, 1889, Oberwesel; Jewish, m; teacher; last German residence: Offenbach, 1940: London.

The author comes from a lower-middle-class family of butchers and learns a trade before becoming a teacher in a small Hessian village. He experiences very little antisemitism and remembers village life fondly. At a second job in the town of Offenbach, he becomes more involved in Jewish community life. After the Nazi takeover in 1933 he loses his job and becomes a full-time employee of the Jewish community of Offenbach. After his arrest and incarceration in a concentration camp following *Kristallnacht*, he succeeds in emigrating with his wife.

101 pp., typescript, on microfilm, evaluation.

139. **Liepmann, Rudolf**, 1940: Shanghai.

The file contains only an incomplete evaluation and correspondence indicating that the manuscript was returned to the author.

140. **Linauer, Rudolf von**; 33, b: Trieste; Catholic, divorced; architect; last German residence: Berlin, 1940: Tystberga/Sweden.

A widely traveled architect, the author expresses his astonishment and disgust towards the Nazi movement after returning to Germany in 1934-1935. In a loosely structured, impressionistic manuscript entitled "Inquisition Berlin Alexanderplatz," he describes the process of Nazi takeover and how people around him make their peace with the new regime. Most of the manuscript is taken up with his description of his sudden arrest and incarceration in a concentration camp.

48 pp., typescript.

141. **Linde, Bruno C.**; 47, b: near Posen; Jewish, m, ch: 2 (sons); lawyer; 1940: Portland/Oregon.

The manuscript begins with a lively description of the author's youth as son of a store owner in an East Prussian village. The perceptive descriptions of university life in Berlin and his war service in World War I tie his general political and social observations to the details of everyday life. He works towards his eventual emigration well before 1933 but only leaves for Denmark in 1936, after his legal practice is dissolved.

70 pp., typescript, on microfilm (author not identified by name).

142. **Littauer, Margot**; 22, b: 1917, Posen; Jewish, m; physician's assistant (husband: physician); last German residence: Breslau, 1939: Tel Aviv/Palestine.

Much of this memoir concerns the author's school days during the early 1930s. The infiltration of the Nazis into her school is described at some length, as is the persecution of Jews. As a physician's assistant she witnesses the increasing difficulties of Jewish doctors and the devastation that takes place on *Kristallnacht.* A few weeks later she departs directly for Palestine.

34 pp., typescript.

143. **Litterer, Gisa Bergmann**; b: Vienna; actress, singer; last German residence: Vienna, 1940: New York City.

This lengthy and confused manuscript records the impressions of an aging performer in Vienna's popular musical theater. It contains no chronological information on the historical developments before or after 1933, but includes numerous photographs, programs, and parts of a wide-ranging correspondence.

150 pp., typescript includes photographs and documents.

144. **Loew, Siegfried**; b: 1878, Westerwald (near Koblenz); Jewish, w; dentist; last German residence: Frankfurt am Main, 1940: Jerusalem/Palestine.

The manuscript is a film script entitled "Dschingis Khan," a story of persecution under Nazism based on the experiences of the author's family. Biographical information indicates that the author emigrated to Palestine in 1933.

19 pp., typescript.

145. **Loewenberg, Ernst**; b: [June 15] 1896, Hamburg; Jewish, m, ch: 3 (sons); teacher; last German residence: Hamburg, 1940: Brookline, Massachusetts.

This report focuses on the activism of Hamburg's Jewish community after 1933. The author is a teacher in progressive public schools until 1934 and in Jewish community schools thereafter until his emigration in 1938. He gives a most detailed account of the numerous self-help activities among Hamburg's Jews and provides a general social portrait of that community. He also describes the subtle and the open public pressures on his three sons.

83 pp., typescript, documents; copy in the LBI.

Lit.: Limberg/Rübsaat, Richarz, vol. 3, Röder-Strauss, GV: papers: LBI.

146. **Loewenberg, Ernst.**

This file contains typed copies of letters, excerpts from the author's diary, copies of articles, and pamphlets, articles and speeches by the author, supplementing the memoir in no. 145.

24 items, typed or printed, with index.

147. **Löwith, Karl**; 43, b: 1897, Munich, d: 1973, Heidelberg; Lutheran (Jewish background), m; philosophy professor; last German residence: Marburg: 1940: Sendai/Japan.

The son of a well-to-do Munich painter, the author briefly describes his youth, his army service, and his time as a prisoner in Italy during World War I. After the war he studies philosophy with Eduard Husserl and Martin Heidegger and becomes a professor in Marburg before being removed by the National Socialists. He finds refuge in Rome in 1933/34 and then in Sendai. His memoir, which is chronologically structured, is an intellectual autobiography of considerable depth dealing with the author's development from an apolitical, Nietzschean aesthete to a politically engaged thinker deeply critical of his former teacher, Heidegger.

161 pp., typescript.

Lit.: The manuscript was published posthumously under the title *Mein Leben in Deutschland vor und nach 1933. Ein Bericht* (Stuttgart: Metzler, 1986), Röder/Strauss, GV, NUC. English: *My Life in Germany Before and After 1933: A Report*, trans. Elizabeth King (Urbana: University of Illinois, 1994).

148. **Lohr, Ida Fanny**; b: Sept. 5, 1884, Berlin; Jewish, m, ch: 3; businesswoman; last German residence: Munich, 1940: Bronx/New York.

Originally from a family of small businesspeople in Berlin, the author marries the owner of a retail store in Munich, where she raises a family in the 1920s and 1930s. Her impressions are chronologically organized and concern large-scale political events only in passing, concentrating instead on the effects of war, revolution, economic deprivation and the rise of Nazism on the life of a businesswoman and mother of three children. The manuscript also describes her arrest and incarceration by the Nazis.

103 pp., typescript, evaluation.

149. **Mann, Edith Weiss**; b: 1885, Hamburg; Jewish, m, ch: 1 (son); professor of education, journalist; last German residence: Hamburg, 1940: New York City.

This memoir opens with recollections of the author's school days and her education at the University of Berlin. Most of her story, however, focuses on her experiences as a professor of music education at the teachers' college in Hamburg. The memoir also deals with the musical life of the 1920s and 1930s and the gradual domination of Nazi teachers in the hierarchy of teacher education. The author becomes a journalist and foreign correspondent on musical affairs for the *Frankfurter Zeitung* in 1933 and resides abroad until 1937, when she returns to Germany to be with her son, who is also a musician. Together they emigrate to New York City in 1939. Her narrative shows her to be quite unaffected in her personal life by antisemitism; she emigrates mainly because her son's future as a musician can only be fulfilled abroad.

116 pp., handwritten, on microfilm (poor quality), evaluation.

150. **Mannes, Bruno**; b: 1899, Oederau/Saxony; Jewish; judge and university professor; last German residence: Dresden, 1939: Isle of Man, British internment camp; 1940: London/England.

This brief, matter-of-fact memoir describes the author's childhood in Wilhelmine Germany as well as politics in Saxony during the early 1920s. As a university student, judge and (after 1928) professor at the University of Leipzig he observes antisemitism early on. He is able to continue as legal advisor and private teacher until 1935, when he flees to Prague and, in May of 1939, to Great Britain.

44 pp., handwritten.

151. Marcus, Ernst; b: 1890, Breslau, [d: Dec. 31, 1982, San Francisco]; Jewish, m; lawyer; last German residence: Breslau, 1940: New York City, later Los Angeles/California.

This detailed and perceptive memoir begins with remembrances of the author's childhood in Wilhelmine Germany as the son of comfortably middle-class parents. After service in World War I and close contact with a range of more proletarian Germans in the army, the author observes the workings of the judicial system in his hometown during the Weimar years. As a lawyer he closely witnesses the Nazi takeover of the judicial system. Under Nazi rule the author defends some political prisoners. In the second half of the memoir the author adds his observations of peoples' relationship to National Socialism as an ideology and organization.

130 pp., typescript, evaluation; copy in the LBI, English translation in the LBI.

Lit.: Limberg/Rübsaat; papers: LBI.

152. Marx, Otto; 50; Jewish, m, ch: 1; merchant; last German residence: Weiden/Oberpfalz, 1940: New York City.

In this brief account the author, formerly the owner of a men's clothing store on the Czech-German border, tells the story of his arrest and imprisonment in Dachau. Released in 1935, he succeeds in emigrating to the United States in 1938.

14 pp., typescript, includes documents.

153. Meiers, J.; 42, b: Berlin; Jewish, w; owner of medical laboratory; last German residence: Berlin, 1940: Belmar/New Jersey.

An activist in the revolution of 1918-19 and a former medic in Moscow, the author briefly recounts his life until 1933. He leaves Germany in the summer of that year. The memoir recounts these events in fragmentary, notebook style. There is no continuous narrative.

7 pp., typescript and handwritten.

154. Meissner, Kurt; 68; editor of *Neues Wiener Journal*; last German residence: Vienna, 1939: Paris/France.

The file contains no memoir, but rather the manuscript of a novel entitled "Die Sintflut" dealing with the decline of the Austrian republic during the 1920s and early 1930s. It contains no personal information. In a brief introduction the author asserts that he belonged to a circle of artists in Vienna that included Arthur Schnitzler, Gustav Mahler, and Herrmann Bahr.

197 pp., typescript, evaluation.

155. Menzel, Rudolfine; b: 1891, Vienna; Jewish, m; dog trainer (husband: physician); last German residence: Linz, 1940: near Haifa/Palestine.

This extensive account by a woman with an unusual career describes her youth in a well-to-do Viennese family and the gradual growth of her Zionist consciousness. Her observations on dogs, scientists, Social Democracy and other topics reveal her to be a believer in *völkisch* ideas about race and an upper-class eccentric. She emphasizes the personal friendship with many Germans she knew throughout the 1930s.

261 pp., typescript, evaluation.

156. Merecki, Siegfried; 52; Jewish, m, ch: 3 (daughters); lawyer; last German residence: Vienna, 1940: Cleveland/Ohio.

This detailed and systematic report provides little information on Austria before the *Anschluss*. Most of the memoir concerns the politics and personal terror thereafter. Special emphasis is placed on the legal regulations limiting Jewish participation in daily life, the fate of lawyers and physicians, deportations, and the author's own lengthy attempt to to emigrate. He departs for the United States on Nov. 10, 1938.

125 pp., typescript.

157. **"Mibberlin, Rafael"** (pseudonym); b: 1893, Berlin; Jewish, m, ch: 1 (daughter); ophthalmologist; last German residence: Berlin, 1940: San Francisco/California.

Raised in an observant Jewish family, the author describes his school experiences and university years. He becomes a Zionist but remains in Germany after military service in World War I to become a medical resident at a university hospital. During the 1920s and early 1930s he has a medical practice in a medium-sized town in Southeastern Germany. He includes observations about Eastern European Jews in Germany as well as his experiences as a doctor under National Socialist rule.

82 pp., typescript.

Lit.: Limberg/Rübsaat.

158. **Miedzwinski, Gerhard**; 28, b: 1911, Kattowitz; Jewish, s; civil engineer; last German residence: Breslau, 1940: Warner's Camp, Seaton/Devon, England.

The author describes his upbringing as a son of a conservative teacher, his university education, and work in the family mining business. The decision to emigrate creates divisions in his family.

16 pp., typescript, in English.

159. **Moses, Hugo**; b: 1895; Jewish, m, ch: 2 (son, daughter); businessman; last German residence: small industrial town in the Ruhr area, 1940: Rochester/New York.

The short memoir describes the conservative author's work for a bank, his persecution after 1933, and his subsequent imprisonment as well as his views on gentile-Jewish relations (which he sees as harmonious prior to 1933). The account includes a description of everyday life after 1933, his imprisonment in the wake of *Kristallnacht* and his flight.

20 pp., typescript, evaluation.

Lit.: Limberg/Rübsaat.

160. **Moses, Margaret**; b: late 1890s, South Germany; Jewish, m, ch: 2 (sons); music teacher (husband: university professor); last German residence: Berlin, 1940: Tel Aviv/Palestine.

The manuscript is not a memoir, but an untitled novella about a Jewish family's life after 1933. Persecution, discriminatory laws and a general discussion of the decline of German culture play an important role. The story does not reflect the author's background as a Zionist and Social Democrat (as indicated in a biographical sketch).

81 pp., typescript.

161. **Munk, Erich**; 1940: Zurich.

This memoir is an account of the life of a close relative; it contains no biographical data on the author himself, but gives a rather detailed description of the unnamed protagonist's life. He is the son of a wealthy businessman and studies law during the Weimar years. A well-established attorney, he loses his livelihood and social position after 1933 and is unable to cope with this loss. He leaves the country temporarily, leaving behind his family only to return to the parental home. In the wake of *Kristallnacht* he is imprisoned and dies in a concentration camp.

25 pp., typescript.

162. **Nathorff, Hertha**; b: June 5, 1895 [d. 1993: New York]: Laupheim/Württemberg; Jewish, m, ch: 1; physician, later nurse; last German residence: Berlin, 1940: New York City.

This entry contains a ten-page introductory narrative of the author's life as a child of middle-class parents, a medical student, and a Social Democratic hospital physician during the Weimar years. The rest of the manuscript is an engagingly written diary transcript starting with January 30, 1933. The diary focuses on the daily and increasingly restricted life of a lively and open-minded woman physician in Nazi Berlin. The diary continues through *Kristallnacht*, during which her husband is incarcerated. It covers most of 1939 and ends with her exile in London.

72 pp., typescript, $15 prizewinner.

Lit.: published as part of *Das Tagebuch der Hertha Nathorff. Berlin-New York, Aufzeichnungen 1933-1945*, (Munich: Oldenbourg, 1987), ed. Wolfgang Benz; Röder/Strauss.

163. **Necheles-Magnus, Henrietta**; b: July 7, 1898, Berlin; m, ch: 2; physician (husband: physician); last German residence: Wandsbek; 1940: Chicago/Illinois.

The memoir of this physician from a comfortable family deals with her student years during World War I and her success at building up a medical practice for women and children after 1924 in Hamburg. She and her husband attempt to continue practicing medicine, but after her second child is born she decides instead to emigrate with her family. The manuscript focuses on the daily life of a family physician in the 1920s and 1930s and also provides lively descriptions of a hospital doctor's everyday life.

26 pp., typescript, evaluation, includes typed copies of documents and letters.

Lit.: Limberg/Rübsaat

164. **Neumann, Martha**; 39, b: Dresden; m, ch: 1 (son); stenographer, typist (husband: electrician); last German residence: Dresden, 1940: Visby/Sweden.

Written from the perspective of a working-class wife whose husband is active in Dresden city politics as a socialist, the report describes the rise of antisemitism and electoral politics before and after 1933. This is the second of two reports sent; the first one is missing.

119 pp., handwritten.

165. **Neumann, Siegfried**; 45, b: Brandenburg; Jewish, m, ch: 2 (son, daughter); lawyer; last German residence: Brandenburg, 1940: Shanghai, later: Palestine.

This precise and insightful memoir covers the author's childhood in Wilhelmine Prussia and his university years and military service in World War I. He focuses on the disintegration of the state as a legal entity in the 1930s. The latter part of the manuscript includes a description of his arrest, concentration camp imprisonment, and emigration. The author's insights are those of a lawyer concerned about the legal framework of democratic life.

121 pp., typescript, evaluation.

Lit.: Limberg/Rübsaat. Manuscript was published as: *Nacht über Deutschland: Vom Leben und Sterben einer Republik. Ein Tatsachenbericht* (Munich: List, 1978); notes indicate that the manuscript was also published in Palestine.

166. **Neustätter, Otto**; 69; Jewish, m; physician; last German residence: Berlin, 1940: Baltimore/Maryland.

Raised in an Orthodox Jewish family, the author begins his memoir with a description of his background and his decision to join the Ethical Culture movement and to study gynecology. The second half of the manuscript deals with his activism as an organizer of exhibitions on public health and women in the early 1930s, his observations on the changing public health profession, and his analysis of the appeal of fascist culture to a wide variety of classes. The manuscript gives a broad picture of daily life under the Nazis from the viewpoint of a middle-class professional.

86 pp., typescript.

167. Nielsen, Borge; 26; Lutheran, s; employee of grain merchant; last German residence: Hamburg, 1940: Chicago/Illinois.

A Danish citizen who lived and worked in Germany from 1936 to 1938, the author describes his impressions of Germany during that time. His portrait of Nazi Germany is impressionistic and neutral.

75 pp., typescript, in English.

168. Nord, Walter; 61, b: Schwerin; Jewish, m, ch: 3; lawyer; last German residence: Hamburg, 1940: Chicago/Illinois.

The memoir contains factual though general observations on German politics, law, and the fate of democratic culture from the viewpoint of an upper-class lawyer and democrat. The author follows a broadly chronological line and separates personal chapters from the more numerous general observations which focus on the decline of the democratic state under National Socialism.

109 pp., typescript, evaluation.

169. Nothdurft, Erich, 30; Protestant; clerk; last German residence: Berlin, 1940: Westfield/New Jersey.

The author recounts his student years in the early 1930s as an essentially apolitical observer. He works part-time for the NSDAP, becomes an army recruit and later an employee of a government office. His somewhat naive and apolitical account of life inside Nazi Germany makes his decision to emigrate look incongruous.

30 pp., typescript on microfilm.

170. "Old Glory" (pseudonym of female author); 38, b: Bavarian town of 420,000; Lutheran, s; stenographer, typist.

The short report contains a description of the Nazi seizure of power in the author's hometown.

7 pp., handwritten.

171. **Oppenheimer, Mara**; b: 1898, Cologne; Jewish, m, ch: 2; housewife (husband: salesman); last German residence: Cologne, 1940: San Francisco/California.

The short memoir focuses on the author's rather undisturbed family life before 1938 and the rude awakening that she and her family face as her husband is about to lose his job and they are forced to emigrate.

10 pp., typescript.

172. **Oppler, Alfred Christian**; b: Feb. 19, 1893, Alsace-Lorraine; Protestant (Jewish parents), m, ch: 1 (daughter); judge; last German residence: Berlin, 1940: Cambridge/Massachusetts.

From a middle-class, conservative family of assimilated Jews in Alsace-Lorraine, the author is unaware of his Jewish ancestry until he is twelve. After legal studies in Berlin and military service in World War I, he observes the disintegration of the Weimar Republic from the viewpoint of a successful jurist and civil servant. He joins the National Socialist Party after 1933 and continues to remain undisturbed by the developments around him even after his demotion from his position as a superior court judge. His dismissal from the civil service in 1936 puts him in a difficult legal and political position which he describes in some detail. After lengthy waits and struggles, he succeeds in attaining an immigration visa to the US in 1939.

90 pp., typescript, evaluation.

Lit.: Röder/Strauss.

173. **Ottenheimer, Elsie**; b: 1894, Munich; Jewish, m, ch: 2; writer, journalist; last German residence: Stuttgart 1940: Altoona/Pennsylvania.

From an industrial family, the author grows up in a small town in Württemberg. Her manuscript hews close to personal autobiography. Most of her report describes incidents of Nazi persecution and a description of National Socialist policies, although not in a chronological or analytical fashion.

46 pp., typescript.

174. **Paeschke, Carl**; b: Oct 17, 1895, Krieschht/Neumark; Protestant, s; journalist; last German residence: Reiboldsgrün, 1940: Zurich.

A sensitive child, the author grows up as the son of small industrialists who lose their factory. After service in World War I, he joins the SPD and becomes a journalist and party activist in Upper Silesia; in 1933 he emigrates to Switzerland. An impressionistic writer, whose narrative is characterized by much psychoanalytic evaluation, the author also provides a detailed account of Social Democratic activism in the working-class districts of Upper Silesia.

57 pp., typescript, evaluation, wins half of first prize ($250).

Lit.: Röder/Strauss.

175. **Papenek-Akselried, Rose Marie**; b: 1904; Jewish, m; journalist; last German residence: Vienna, 1940: Cincinnati/Ohio.

As the daughter of a well-known Viennese newspaper editor, the author witnesses the political unrest of the 1920s there. Although she receives a university degree in agriculture, she works as a journalist in the 1930s and marries a book publisher. The matter-of-fact memoir contains descriptions of the rise of antisemitism and the Nazi takeover of Austria.

105 pp., typescript, on microfilm, evaluation.

176. **Paschkis, Victor**; b: 1898, Vienna [d: June 18, 1991, Frederick/Pennsylvania]; Catholic [later Quaker] grandparents: Jewish; engineer; 1940: Hamden/Connecticut.

This brief, factual memoir contains a description of the author's family and education in Catholic schools, his service in World War I, and the hardship and political chaos of Berlin and Vienna after World War I. As a consulting engineer, he travels widely throughout Europe beginning in the late 1920s and makes his home base in Holland and Italy after 1934, but continues to visit Germany until his emigration in 1938.

28 pp., typescript, in English, evaluation.

Lit.: Röder/Strauss; *The New York Times*, June 20, 1991.

177. **Pfeffer, Gerta**; b: 1912, Saxony; Jewish, s; textile designer, now working as maid; last German residence: small town in Southwest Germany, 1940: London.

The daughter of a Chemnitz businessman, the author gets her first job in a small textile mill in rural Southwest Germany. In lively vignettes she describes the social and political makeup of the town and the deterioration of the social climate after 1936. Expelled to Poland in the late 1930s, she leaves the continent to work as a maid in England in 1939.

62 pp., typescript.

Lit.: Limberg/Rübsaat.

178. **Polke, Max Moses**; b: 1896, Breslau; Jewish, m, ch: 3; lawyer; last German residence: Breslau, 1940: Petach-Tikvah/Palestine.

A lifetime resident of Breslau until his emigration in the late 1930s, the author has an early awareness of antisemitism. He becomes a Zionist, and his descriptions of Zionism and 1920s culture and media are particularly lively. As an activist democrat and liberal lawyer, he is an early target of Nazi hostility. After acting as defense attorney in *Rassenschande* cases, he is arrested and deported to Buchenwald concentration camp. The memoir contains detailed, insightful descriptions of the Gestapo machinery of terror.

150 pp., typescript, $5 prizewinner.

This file also contains the following correspondence: unsigned announcements of $20.00 prize to K. Frankenthal (Nov. 12, 1940), $10.00 to Kuno Fiedler (Nov. 12, 1940, from Hartshorne), $5.00 to Max Polke (March 2, 1941), $20.00 to Arthur Samuel (Nov. 14, 1940), $20.00 to Edward Heilpern, and $10 to Richard Wolf.

Lit.: Limberg/Rübsaat; papers: LBI.

179. **Popper, Lotte**; b: November 28, 1898, Preussisch Stargard/East Prussia; Jewish, m, ch: 3; high school science teacher (husband: dentist); last German residence: Hamburg, 1940: Tel Aviv.

The author comes from an orthodox Jewish background and describes the life of an observant family in Hamburg. The husband's dental practice brings her into daily contact with non-Jewish working-class patients, and her detailed description of the family members' interaction with this group and with one another make it an especially lively account. The family leaves for Palestine in 1936.

87 pp., typescript. The file also contains a sheet: "criteria for selecting the prize-winning manuscript."

Lit.: Richarz, vol. 2 contains an excerpt of a later memoir by this author.

180. **R., Mrs. J. S.**; 1940: New York City.

The file contains no memoir, but rather a brief report by the (anonymous) Mrs. R. on her son, a theology student in Germany. She deplores the anti-Christian nature of the Nazi regime.

5 pp., handwritten, in English.

181. **Rathgeber, Ernst**; 34, b: Kassel; Protestant, s; writer, editorial assistant; last German residence: Stuttgart, 1939: Leeds/England, later:

Australia.

A self-educated writer, the author describes his youth as an apprentice and member of socialist youth groups. The memoir chronicles the author's education in night school and his perceptive observations of everyday life in the 1930s. He leaves Germany in early 1939.

23 pp., typescript.

182. **Reiner, Max**; b: March 23, 1883, Czernovitz/Bukowina [d: 1944, Jerusalem]; Jewish, m; journalist, editor; last German residence: Berlin, 1940: Jerusalem.

A well-known Berlin journalist and editor for Ullstein publishing house, the author begins his lengthy and lively memoir with a description of Berlin and its culture before and after 1914. War and revolution, the inflation, and the Hitler Putsch take up the first half of the manuscript. Later the author turns to the politics of m
of power. Although these events and the developments up to 1936 are described impressionistically, the memoir provides a vivid and detailed history of the period. Much of the memoir is based on the author's diaries.

254 pp., typescript, evaluation; copy in the LBI.

Lit.: Limberg/Rübsaat; Richarz, vol.2; Röder/Strauss; papers: LBI.

183. **Reinheimmer, Dr. Hans**; Catholic, m; physicist; last German residence: Berlin, 1940: Boston/Massachusetts.

This brief account focuses on the author's dismissal from his job as a scientist in a factory after denunciations by a Nazi sympathizer. He also describes his odyssey from England to Argentina and finally to the United States.

13 pp., typescript, in English, evaluation.

184. Reuss, Dr. F. S.; 35; Catholic (Jewish background), m, ch: 1 (son); economist with German state railroad system; last German residence: Berlin, 1940: Loretto/Pennsylvania (later, New Orleans/Louisiana).

In this perceptive memoir, the author focuses on the decay of upper-class German society during the 1930s. As the son of a judge, he enjoys a comfortable pre-war childhood but then witnesses the ravages of inflation and economic distress. During his years as a high-level railroad official, he travels through Germany and Europe observing moods and opinions of the upper class. The manuscript is particularly interesting for its observations on foreigners and their relationship to Germany.

62 pp., typescript, evaluation.

Lit.: Röder/Strauss.

185. Richter, Werner; [b: July 1, 1888, Muskau; d: Aug. 14, 1969; Protestant; journalist, writer; 1940: Switzerland]: 1941: Elmhurst/Illinois.

The file contains no manuscript, but only some correspondence.

Lit.: Röder/Strauss, GV.

186. Rie, Dr. Robert; b: 1904, Vienna; Lutheran (Jewish background); lawyer and writer; last German residence: Vienna, 1940: Washington, D.C.

The manuscript consists of an unpublished work entitled "Der Europamüde." It describes the author's last two weeks in Vienna after the German takeover; it also follows him to exile in Paris and the United States, where life among refugees is described in witty detail.

237 pp., typescript.

187. Riederer, Willibald; b: 1868; craftsman; 1940: Chicago/Illinois.

A working-class immigrant who came to the U. S. in 1886, the author reminisces about his childhood in Germany and his positive impressions on visiting again in 1890 and 1935.

10 pp., handwritten, evaluation.

188. Rodeck, Frederick; b: 1890, Vienna; Jewish, m; journalist; last German residence: Vienna, 1940: Pontiac/Michigan.

This lengthy report recounts the author's general impressions of the origins of National Socialism, the takeover of Austria, subsequent changes in public life, and the persecution of Jews. Observations on Austria's legal and economic structures under Nazi rule are also part of the account, which contains little biographical information. The author contends that the majority of Austrians, especially members of the upper class, were outraged by the Nazi takeover.

156 pp., typescript, evaluation.

189. Rodenbaeck, Louise+.

An American, the author first travels to Hamburg as a student in 1912 and revisits in 1933, 1934, and 1937. Her observations mainly concern everyday life. She closely examines several *Schrebergarten* colonies and youth organizations. Her impressions of Germany under the Nazis are distant and somewhat favorable. She does not mention the growth of antisemitism.

96 pp., typescript, in English, on microfilm, filed out of order.

190. Rosenmann, Wilhelmine; b: 1891, Nuremberg; Jewish, widowed, ch: 2; housewife; last German residence: Munich, 1940: Youngstown/Ohio.

This short report gives a brief biographical sketch of the author's life as wife of a businessman and her difficulties after his death in 1932.

5 pp., typescript.

191. Rosenthal, Henry; 48; Jewish, m; last German residence: Berlin; 1940: Shanghai.

This brief report describes the author's army service and comfortable life before World War I; he loses his money in the inflation of the early 1920s. The manuscript also contains general observations on Germany since 1933.

2 pp., typescript.

192. Rosenthal, Karl; 55, b: a village in Teutoburger Wald; Jewish, m, ch: 2 (sons); rabbi; last German residence: Berlin, 1940: Oxford/England.

The author, chief rabbi of the Reform synagogue in Berlin, describes a happy childhood in rural Germany and then focuses on his role as a leader of Berlin's Reform Jews after 1933. He is arrested in 1938. Most of his memoir describes his concentration camp experience in Sachsenhausen.

123 pp., typescript, evaluation; papers: LBI.

193. Rosenthal, Walter; b: 1873, Berlin; Jewish, m, ch: 1 (daughter); lawyer; last German residence: Berlin, 1940: Brookline/Massachusetts.

This straightforward biographical account gives the story of the author's youth and student days and then focuses on the development of the legal profession before and after World War I. He also discusses the position of Jews in the legal and judicial system and their persecution after 1933.

61 pp., typescript, evaluation.

194. **Sakheim, Leon** (pseudonym: "**Leon Rumagra**"); b: 1904, Hamburg; Jewish; 1940: Boston/Massachusetts.

The manuscript is an essay entitled "Nietzsche over Europe," in which the author proposes that National Socialism is an amalgamation of Prussian traditions and Nietzschean ideas. The essay contains no biographical information.

18 pp., typescript, evaluation. The file contains an extensive evaluation and notes of an interview with the author.

Lit.: NUC.

195. **Salzburg, Friedrich,** b: June 4, 1874, Dresden; Jewish, m, ch: 4 (3 sons, 1 daughter); lawyer; last German residence: Dresden, 1940: Berkeley/California.

The author comes from a middle-class family of Dresden Jews and after school and university years builds up a successful legal practice in his hometown. He is drafted at age forty into wartime duty, but is able to rebuild his legal practice during the Weimar years and leads the comfortable and well-integrated life of an upper-middle-class professional. After the Nazi takeover his professional existence is slowly stripped away. Although he retains some social standing, he decides to follow one of his children to the United States. The manuscript contains noteworthy insights into the legal and court system and the emigration process.

114 pp., typescript, on microfilm, evaluation. The file includes documents (typed copies and originals).

196. **Samuel, Arthur**; b: 1886, Bonn, [d: 1974, USA]; Jewish, m, ch: 2 (sons); physician; last German residence: Bonn, 1940: New York City.

This biographical account begins with the author's childhood and wartime memories. Despite numerous experiences with antisemitism at school and university, he succeeds in building a successful medical practice in Bonn by the early 1930s. He becomes a leader of the Jewish community there and is immediately the target of a boycott after 1933. The memoir describes in some detail the harassment, imprisonment and torture of the author and other Jews of his hometown. After losing his medical license, he flees via Switzerland to the United States.

50 pp., typescript evaluation, documents; copy in the LBI.

Lit.: Limberg/Rübsaat.

197. Sass, Karl; Jewish, m, ch: 1; religion teacher; last German residence: Vienna, 1940: Kitchener Camp, Richborough/England.

The memoir concentrates on the author's experience before and after the Austrian *Anschluss.* He is arrested and succeeds in fleeing to England. The manuscript contains a lively and detailed description of the persecution of Viennese Jews and their attempts to flee abroad clandestinely with the help of paid smugglers.

30 pp., typescript.

198. Saunders, Anna; b: 1888, Germany; Baptist, w; housewife, governess; 1940: Richmond/Virginia.

The German-born author emigrates to the United States in 1910. After her husband's death she returns from 1936 to 1938. Her report enthusiastically endorses the changes in Germany during the 1930s.

20 pp., typescript, evaluation.

199. Schapira, David; b: 1898; Jewish; physician; last German residence: Vienna, 1940: London.

The report briefly describes life in Vienna and the author's deportation to Dachau and Buchenwald after the *Anschluss.*

7 pp., typescript.

200. Scherzer, Oskar; b: Dec 31, 1920, Elbing/East Prussia; Jewish; college student; last German residence: Elbing, 1940: Bronx/New York.

The memoir, prepared as a book manuscript, weaves the story of the author's life as a high school student with the description of his first love, a non-Jewish fellow student. While he prepares to leave the country, his father is depor a n t i c . e v d r i a d o e detailed impressions of the everyday life of a teenager and young student.

135 pp., typescript.

201. Schloss, Oscar; b: 1875 Heidelberg; Jewish, m; manufacturer; last German residence: Frankfurt/Main, 1940: New York City.

In this detailed memoir, which was completed before the contest announcement, the author describes his childhood and World War I service in the Austrian army. Otherwise, he spends little time on the circumstances of his life and work as an adult prior to 1933, but focuses on life under Nazi rule. He describes his emigration via Great Britain (where members of his family live) to the U.S.

150 pp., typescript, in English.

202. Schmidt, Gerhard; 37; Jewish, s; [businessman; last German residence: Berlin].

This brief memoir describes the author's university years and his work in the family business, which is increasingly threatened by the Nazis. In the wake of *Kristallnacht* he is arrested and put into a concentration camp. After his dismissal he emigrates to China in the spring of 1939.

19 pp., typescript, evaluation; papers: LBI.

203. Schneider, Helene; 40; Jewish, divorced, ch: 2; social worker; last German residence: a North German city, 1940: Bedford Hills/New York.

The author is a social worker in public service until her dismissal in 1933; she then works for Jewish welfare agencies until her two-year imprisonment in a concentration camp for hiding a labor leader. The manuscript focuses on her concentration camp experience and provides interesting reflections on psychological adjustment and survival tactics, especially of women prisoners.

104 pp., typescript, evaluation.

204. Schreier, Fritz; b: 1897, Vienna; Jewish, m, ch: 1 (son); lawyer; last German residence: Vienna, 1940: Geneva/Switzerland.

This account is a detailed description of the author's arrest in March 1938, deportation, and imprisonment in Dachau and Buchenwald concentration camps. The report is insightful and analytical.

42 pp., typescript, original in German, English translation included (24 pp.).

205. Schubert, Franziska; 48, b: Vienna; Protestant, m, (husband: Jewish); actress; 1940: New York City.

This memoir, by a successful theater actress, chronicles her childhood, her early successes and work with Max Reinhardt, and her career during the 1920s, which takes her from the German provinces to Berlin. Her observations link personal incidents and encounters with theater people under Nazi rule with general observations on political developments.

83 pp., typescript, evaluation.

206. Schürmann, Fritz; b: January 8, 1915, Hildesheim; Jewish, s; tailor; last German residence: Hildesheim; 1940: Kitchener Camp,

Ritchborough/England.

As son of the owner of a large men's tailoring store, the author is trained to succeed his father, but has to flee after his arrest and temporary imprisonment in Buchenwald. Much of the account focuses on his experiences in the concentration camp. He also describes his attempts to gain admission to the United States.

22 pp., typescript.

Lit.: Limberg/Rübsaat; papers: LBI.

207. **Schwabe, Karl**; 48, b: Hanau; Jewish, m, ch: 2; owned department store; 1939: London, 1941: Philadelphia/Pennsylvania.

The memoir is written in chronological order and begins with a description of the home front during World War I. In this well-written account, the events of 1919, the Weimar years, and the rise of Hitler are reported from the perspective of a small-town businesman. The author makes plans to emigrate, but succeeds only after a period of imprisonment in Buchenwald concentration camp.

90 pp., typescript; copy in the LBI.

208. **Schwartz, Oscar** [b: 1880, Bucharest; Jewish; lawyer, legal counsel; last German residence: Berlin, 1939: London].

The file contains no manuscript; available in the LBI.

Lit.: Richarz, vol. 2; Röder/Strauss.

209. **Schwartzert, Ernst**; 34; Protestant, m, (wife: Jewish); playwright; 1940: New Rochelle/New York.

The author describes his middle-class youth as the son of a well-to-do North German merchant. Before embarking on a career as a sometimes successful playwright, he finishes an apprenticeship in a factory. Most of the memoir records the author's insightful observations on intellectuals' relationships to Nazis and the general intellectual climate of the 1930s. His decision to emigrate is hastened by his encounter with an American Jew and his friendship with a Jewish woman in Germany (later his wife).

91 pp., typescript. The researchers urged the author to send parts of the manuscript to *Harper's Magazine* or *The Atlantic Monthly*.

210. Shiller, Hettie; b: 1906, Berlin, (d: July, 1940); Jewish, m, ch: 1 (daughter); dietitian, psychologist (husband: judge); last German residence: Berlin, 1940: Cleveland/Ohio.

This lively, rather discontinuous account has two parts. The first focuses on the author's happy childhood, her impressions of World War I on the homefront, her student years, and her life as a young wife. The second part describes her everyday life in the 1930s, Nazi oppression, and her short stay in Palestine, followed by her return to Germany. In a dramatic escape she and her husband are able to emigrate to the United States in 1938.

100 pp., typescript, pp.1-49 on microfilm; receives a special $10 prize.

Lit.: Limberg/ Rübsaat.

211. Short, Howard Elmo; 32; Protestant, s; minister; last German residence: Marburg, 1940: Cuyahoga Falls/Ohio.

The author was an American student of theology at the University of Marburg in 1932/1933. As a graduate student he lived in a student dormitory with Germans. He provides impressions of political activities of fellow students, professors, and the Nazi takeover after the election of 1933. The final part of the manuscript explores the author's views on theology, with little connection to the preceding account.

Approximately 60 pp. (final page or pages missing), typescript, in English.

212. Sichel, Hilda Honnet; b: 1888, Pine Bluff/Arkansas; Jewish, m, ch: 2; language teacher (husband: lawyer); last German residence: Frankfurt am Main, 1940: Boston/Massachusetts.

The author, an American, leaves her hometown in Arkansas after high school to study in Vienna and Berlin in 1909. She describes the intellectual and cultural life in the two cities and gives a generally critical and distant view of the German social order. She marries a German lawyer but remains distant from the political developments of the 1920s and 1930s until her husband's career is destroyed and he is arrested and put into a concentration camp. The author describes in some detail her struggle with German and American consular authorities, which eventually leads to freedom and emigration for her and her family.

112 pp., typescript, in English, evaluation.

Lit.: Limberg/Rübsaat.

213. Siemsen, Anna; b: Jan. 18, 1882, Mark/Westfalen [d: Jan. 22, 1952, Hamburg]; Protestant, s; educator, politician; 1940: Chexbres/Switzerland.

The daughter of a minister, the author attends university to study German literature and is an acute observer of the Prussian educational system. She becomes a socialist and joins the USPD in 1919 and the SPD in 1922. Her insights into the politics of education continue as she moves into a career as an educational administrator and university teacher and as a city councilwoman. Because of r l c a l i s l s r o s h i 9 n she emigrates in 1933, th i period.

86 pp., typescript.

Lit.: Röder/Strauss, NUC, GV, August Siemsen, *Anna Siemsen, Leben und Werk* (Hamburg and Frankfurt: Europaische Verlagsanstalt, 1951).

214. Silberpfennig, Henda.

The file contains no manuscript.

215. Solon, Friedrich; b: 1882 [d: 1952, London]; Jewish; lawyer; last German residence: Berlin, 1940: England.

The file contains no manuscript. Evaluation; available in the LBI.

Lit.: Richarz, vols. 2 and 3, Limberg/Rübsaat; papers: LBI.

216. Solon, Fritz; 1940: London/England.

The manuscript is a book-length treatise entitled "Panorama: A Philosophical System." It contains no biographical information or historical observations. The author is probably the same person as the author of no. 215. Both books contain a short portion of an autobiographical manuscript by the author.

Approximately 300 pp., typescript.

217. Sorkin, Karl (Charles); 32, b: Basel; Jewish, m, (wife: Protestant) ch:1; clerk, grocery store owner, chess player; last German residence: Freiburg 1940: Akron/Ohio.

From a lower-middle-class family in Basel, the author recalls an unhappy childhood and better years as a young bank clerk. An amateur chess player, he recounts his days as a traveling champion in Germany in the 1920s and 1930s as well as his increasingly difficult life as owner of a grocery store. He separates from his wife and emigrates to the United States in 1938.

79 pp., typescript, evaluation; the file also contains an undergraduate paper analyzing the manuscript.

218. **Spera, Helen Hirsch**; b: April 13, 1897, Klosterneuburg; Jewish, s; translator; last German residence: Vienna, 1940: New York City.

From an upper-middle-class home, the author studies languages at university but has to go to work to support the family after her father's death. Her description of life in Austria before 1938 shows little awareness of the rise of fascism, but after the *Anschluss* she is subject to humiliation and persecution. The final third of the manuscript describes her emigration to the United States and her first impressions of life there.

81 pp., typescript.

219. **Spiegel, Margot**; b: April 27, 1914, Konstanz; student, Jewish; s; 1940: Grand Rapids/Michigan.

The daughter of assimilated Jews in South Germany, the author only becomes aware of her heritage as Nazi persecution of Jews intensifies after 1933. The memoir describes an increasing sense of isolation from non-Jewish peers and intensified study of religion and Zionism with Jewish friends. After some conflict with her beleaguered father, who refuses to leave, she goes to the United States as an au-pair and remains there as a student of home economics. By 1940 her parents are deported to Gurs internment camp.

50 pp., typescript, in English.

220. **Spiegel, Walter**; 52; Protestant, (grandparents Jewish), m; teacher; last German residence: North German town: 1940: Vicksburg/ Mississippi.

A comfortably assimilated son of middle-class parents, the author focuses on Christian-Jewish relations from the Wilhelmine era until the rise of National Socialism. From the viewpoint of a Gymnasium teacher he pays special attention to school life and church life. The last third of the manuscript contains a detailed description of the author's sufferings in the wake of *Kristallnacht* and his imprisonment in a concentration camp.

Approximately 212 pp. (not consistently numbered), on microfilm.

221. **Spiess, Margarete**; b: Naumburg; 1940: Brooklyn/NY.

The brief report describes the widespread pro-Nazi mood before 1931, when the author emigrates to the United States.

4 pp., handwritten.

222. **Spitz, Reinhold** (pseudonym: "F.H. Reynold"); b: 1873; Jewish, m, ch: 3; factory owner; last German residence: Pullach/Bavaria, 1940: New York City.

A wealthy retired factory owner, the author gives a general description of life during the 1920s and a more specific account of the years from 1933 until his emigration in 1937. Most of the memoir is taken up by personal impressions, not analytical observations.

17 pp., typescript.

223. **Stein, Erica** (pseudonym: "Erica Bond"); b: February 1914, Berlin; Jewish, m; social worker and journalist; last German residence: Berlin, 1940: London/England.

A student at King's College, University of London, the author describes her youth as the daughter of a middle-class family in decline and as a member of socialist groups. She attends a number of public and experimental schools in Berlin and earns money writing newspaper articles while still a high school student. Facing arrest for her socialist activism, she flees in 1933. The memoir is well written and provides detailed insights into the world of left-wing high school students in the late years of Weimar Republic.

19 pp., typescript, in English.

Lit.: Lixl- Purcell.

224. Stein, Herbert (pseudonym: "Tristan Leander"); b: 1909, Vienna; Jewish, s; lawyer, writer; last German residence: Vienna, 1940: Tel Aviv.

The author submitted the manuscript of a novel entitled "Wir Emigranten." Written in mid-1939, before announcements of the essay contest were made, it describes the milieu of upper-class Jewish Vienna in the 1930s and the experiences of emigrants from that world in Palestine. No publication of the novel is known.

493 pp., typescript.

225. Steinbrüchner, Hans; b: June 2, 1912, Thüringen (d: 1940); m; machinist; 1940: Devon/England.

The son of a machinist, the author is unable to continue his education after finishing Gymnasium and becomes a machinist himself. Because of his language skills he works for German firms abroad, but describes the German working class's attitudes towards Hitler as well.

20 pp., handwritten, evaluation. Correspondence indicates that the author died on the torpedoed *Arandora Star* en route to the United States in late 1940.

226. Steiner, Margarete; 48; Jewish, m; bookkeeper (husband: watchmaker); last German residence: Vienna, 1940: Statesville/North Carolina.

The factual memoir describes the author's experiences after the Austrian *Anschluss*. She and her husband are forced to leave their home and business to flee via Italy to Southern France, where her husband is put in an internment camp while she continues to the United States.

35 pp., typescript.

227. Steiner, Rudolf; 38; Jewish, divorced; political activist; last German

residence: Munich and Berlin, 1940: London.

A Communist activist since the early 1920s, the author describes his work on behalf of the unemployed and the KPD during the Weimar years and the increasing political tensions before 1933. He emigrates in the summer of 1934 first to Prague and then, in 1939, via Poland to London. This well-written memoir focuses primarily on the political atmosphere before 1933.

116 pp., typescript, evaluation.

228. Steinfeld, Gerhard, 33, b: Northeastern Germany; Jewish, s; judge, lawyer; last German residence: North German city, 1940: New York.

In this matter-of-fact memoir the author reports briefly on his youth and university studies as well as his service as a judge in various Prussian towns. He is confronted with the disintegration of his professional career and the persecution of his family. After his brother's death in Dachau he emigrates in early 1938.

47 pp., typescript, on microfilm, evaluation.

229. Stern, Fritz; b: Dec. 29, 1892, Vienna; Jewish, m; lawyer; last German residence: Vienna, 1940: New York City.

This sober memoir describes the author's rise from humble origins to respected Social Democratic lawyer in the years after World War I. He is attacked by antisemites as early as 1933, and is a precise observer of the infiltration of Austrian politics and society by the Nazis. After being denied the right to practice law, he leaves for the United States via Sweden in August 1938.

55 pp., typescript, evaluation.

230. Stübs, Albin; b: Feb. 20, 1900, Berlin; Protestant; m, ch: 5; writer,

journalist; 1940: Great Britain.

The file contains no memoir but only correspondence which indicates that the manuscript for a novel, "Die Vandalen," was returned to the author upon request. No publication is known.

Lit.: Röder/Strauss, GV.

231. **Sussman, Walter**; b: June 26, 1918; Jewish; s; university student, last German residence: Vienna, 1940: Louisville/Kentucky.

After a short account of the author's early childhood, the report focuses on the persecution of Jews in Vienna during the days of the *Anschluss* in minute detail. The memoir includes a description of the author's imprisonment and emigration with his family.

73 pp., typescript, on microfilm, in English.

232. **Taut, Lore**; b: 1909; m; office manager (husband: sales representative); 1940: New York City.

The daughter of a Jewish physician and a Protestant mother, the author marries beneath her class and describes the proletarianization of her circumstances after marriage in vivid terms. Both she and her husband are active in Social Democratic circles, and much of the memoir is taken up with descriptions of this world and the workplace of her husband. The memoir contains little specific information on the National Socialists and the circumstances of her emigration.

160 pp., typescript, evaluation.

233. **Thieme, Karl Otto**; b: May 22, 1902, Leipzig [d: July 26, 1963, Basel]; Catholic (convert, previously Lutheran), m, ch: 2 (daughters); university professor, writer; last German residence: Leipzig, 1940: Läufelfingen/Switzerland.

From a family of Protestant theologians, as a young man the author is repulsed by antisemitism and anti-republicanism and joins a religious group of socialists. He is dismissed from his job as a professor at a teachers' college, but continues his activism on behalf of Christian Socialists as a writer and journal editor. A convert to Catholicism in 1935, he goes into exile to continue his activism from Switzerland. Much of this loosely structured memoir focuses on his ideas about how to bring about the downfall of Hitler and the achievement of world peace.

121 pp., evaluation.

Lit.: Röder/Strauss; GV, NUC

234. Tischler, Richard; b: 1882, Breslau; Jewish, m, (wife: Catholic); businessman; 1940: New York City.

This conventional memoir begins with the author's experiences in World War I and then focuses on the Nazi seizure of power. The author is relatively safe almost until the time of his emigration to Yugoslavia in 1934, which is described in some detail.

52 pp., typescript, evaluation.

235. Tobias, Paula; b: 1886, Hamburg; Lutheran, (parents: Jewish), m, ch: 1 (son); physician (husband: physician); last German residence: Bevern/Weser, 1940: Grass Valley/California.

This lengthy and disjointed memoir follows the author's life from her student days in Heidelberg to her years as a country doctor in the vicinity of Braunschweig. Her largely apolitical observations at the beginning give way to reflections on the rise of National Socialism and the role of doctors in the Nazi movement. Numerous documents supplement this narrative.

217 pp., typescript, German and English, includes documents.

236. Vogel, Julius; 36; Protestant, (parents: Jewish); m, writer; last German

residence: Sudetenland, 1940: Noke, Oxfordshire/England.

The entry consists of the manuscript for a novella entitled "We Don't Want Freedom," which describes the slow emergence of radical German nationalism in the author's village in the Erzgebirge. The story contains no autobiographical information.

108 pp., typescript, in English, evaluation.

237. **Vordtriede, Käthe**; [b. Jan. 2, 1891, d. 1964, New York. Hanover; Protestant (Jewish parents), w. ch: 2 (son, daughter); journalist; last German residence: Freiburg im Breisgau, 1940: Switzerland, later: New York.]

In a crisp, analytical account of the years 1924-1933, the author describes the Nazi seizure of power and Germany's gradual transformation. The increasing racialization of society and the persecution of Jews are prominent themes. The memoir concludes with a description of the author's emigration.

116 pp., typescript, on microfilm.

Lit.: the manuscript was published as *Es gibt Zeiten in denen man welkt*, ed. Detlev Garz (Lengwil, Libelle Verlag, 1999).

238. **Walter, Rudolf**; b: 1881, Vienna; Protestant (previously Jewish), m, ch: 1 (son); accountant for railroad company, writer; 1940: Northwood, Middlesex/England.

This short report describes the author's persecution by the Nazis despite his claim that he is a German Christian.

13 pp., typescript.

239. **Weil, Frederick**; b: 1877, Schmieheim/Baden [d: 1953, New York City]; Jewish, m, ch: 5 (2 sons, 3 daughters); wine merchant; last

German residence: Frankfurt am Main, 1940: New York City.

From a Southwest German family of wine and liquor merchants, the author moves to Frankfurt after World War I and becomes active in numerous trade and civic groups. Most of the memoir concerns the period after 1931 and touches on many aspects of life in the Jewish business community amid the rise of Nazism, focusing especially on his experiences as a wine merchant. The author also describes his persecution, arrest, and imprisonment in Buchenwald.

129 pp., typescript; copy in the LBI.

Lit.: Limberg/Rübsaat, Richarz vol. 3.

240. **Weiss, Hilda**; 39, b: Berlin; Jewish, divorced; university researcher and teacher; last German residence: Frankfurt am Main, 1940: Durham/North Carolina.

The author, from an assimilated and politically well-connected family, recounts a very eventful and varied life as a socialist youth and part-time factory worker whose main career as an academic unfolds in the 1920s and early 1930s. Because of her socialist activism, she leaves Germany for Switzerland in April 1933; her report contains no information on her subsequent life abroad.

65 pp., typescript, in English.

241. **Wenzel, Hilde**; Jewish, m, ch: 1 (daughter); book dealer; 1940: Zurich.

The author comes from a comfortable middle-class family. She begins working at an early age in the book business. Most of her account deals with the changes in German society from the mid-1920s to 1938 from the perspective of a book seller and accurate observer of people's reading habits. She emigrates in 1938 to Switzerland via Italy.

37 pp., typescript.

Lit.: Limberg/Rübsaat; papers: LBI.

242. Wilhelm, Dr. Teodoro; about 45, b: Bavaria; Catholic, s; priest, teacher, professional youth leader; 1940: Cali/Colombia.

A strongly anti-Communist and anti-Nazi youth organizer, the author, a Catholic priest, describes his work and his subsequent persecution by the Nazis; he goes first to Czechoslovakia and Austria, and finally to South America.

31 pp., typescript, evaluation.

243. Wolf, Hermann; 59, b: Western Germany; Jewish; lawyer; 1940: New York City.

The manuscript consists of a brief summary of events in Germany before and after 1933.

3 pp., typescript, in English, evaluation.

244. Wolf, Richard; b: 1891, Herford/Westfalia; Protestant, (Jewish ancestry); physician; m., ch: 3, last German residence: Berlin, 1940: Puerto Rico.

From an upper-middle-class family, the author recounts his youth and student years in medical school but also his interest in music and friendships in literary circles. He establishes himself as a physician and starts a family after World War I, but also begins to be aware of increasing antisemitism. He leaves Germany in the fall of 1938. Much of this well-written memoir covers the period before 1933, skillfully blending personal recollection and political events. Despite bitter experiences after 1933, when he is persecuted and finally forced to give up his practice, the author maintains an ironic distance from events.

89 pp., typescript. Parts of the manuscript are typed on poor-quality paper and are difficult to read. According to information in file no. 178, the author received $10.

245. **Wolff, S(?)**; b: 1888; Jewish, divorced; pediatrician; 1940: Rotterdam/Holland.

A former head of a pediatric hospital, the author writes about his youth, student years, and experiences in the hospital in a loosely structured biography. Part of the account focuses on the role of Jewish doctors in Germany in an attempt to refute antisemitic Nazi propaganda.

49 pp., typescript.

246. **Wolff-Arndt, Philippine**; b: Oct 1, 1849, Frankfurt am Main; Protestant, ch: 2; painter; 1939: Paris.

This brief account reviews the varied life of a feminist painter, mainly during the late nineteenth century. The memoir contains little specific information about the post-World War I era.

15 pp., typescript.

247. **Wolfram, Annemarie** (married name: Annemarie Peine); 37, b: Hamburg; Jewish, m, ch: 1 (daughter); kindergarten teacher, nurse (husband: psychologist); 1940: New York City.

The manuscript consists of accounts by three members of the same family, who write from distinct yet complementary viewpoints. Annemarie Wolfram's account contains information about her prosperous Hamburg Jewish family and vignettes which focus on life under Nazi rule, especially after passage of the Nuremberg Laws. Fictional excerpts from her young daughter's diary offer a child's perspective on the experience of persecution and emigration. Her husband discusses his internment in a concentration camp.

50 pp., typescript, evaluation.

Lit.: Lixl-Purcell.

248. Worm, Fritz; 56; Jewish, m, ch: 1 (son); book dealer; last German residence: Lindlar, 1940: Rio de Janeiro.

From a secular family, the author writes about German literature and German culture from an upper-middle-class vantage point. The memoir is interwoven with accounts of his own experiences in the book trade and his persecution after 1933.

96 pp., typescript, on microfilm, evaluation. The manuscript is difficult to read.

249. Wurzel, Herman (pseudonym: "H. Roots"); b: Feb. 19, 1862, W. Prussia; Jewish, ch: 3 (2 sons, 1 daughter); dentist; 1940: Brooklyn/New York.

This memoir contains the general reflections of a retired dentist on Germans in general and West Prussians specifically, as well as comments on his experiences in the army and as a traveler through various European countries. Its accounts of the Nazi seizure of power and life after 1933 are similarly diffuse.

101 pp., handwritten.

250. Wysbar, Eva; 31, Berlin; Jewish, divorced (former husband: Protestant), ch: 2; last German residence: Berlin, 1940: Hollywood/California.

The manuscript has two parts. The first outlines a philosophical treatise on the idea of race and German national character. The second part contains the author's autobiographical memoir of life with her husband, film director Frank Wysbar, and the family's struggle to emigrate. Only after an official divorce do the author and her husband succeed in separately leaving Germany.

48 pp., typescript, evaluation.

Lit.: Limberg/Rübsaat.

251. Yourgrau, Wolfgang (pseudonym: "Dr. Herrmann Tuggelin"); b: Nov. 16, 1908, Kattowitz; Jewish, s; journalist, philosopher; last German residence: Berlin, 1940: Tel Aviv.

The memoir describes the author's childhood in Kattowitz and youth in Berlin, where he studies philosophy and earns a Ph.D. Part of the manuscript deals with the his impressions of Gustav Wyneken, Hermann Hesse, and Ludwig Klages; he also befriends Albert Einstein. He discusses as well his activism as a socialist and the brutal treatment he experiences from Nazis in April 1933. The manuscript does not deal with his experiences after his emigration to Poland in 1933.

52 pp., typescript, evaluation.

Lit.: Röder/Strauss; Limberg/Rübsaat ("Hermann Tuggelin").

252. Zeitlin, Egon; b: March 3, 1901, Leipzig [d. 1965, Frankfurt am Main]; Jewish, m., ch: 2 (son and daughter); lawyer; last German residence: Berlin, 1940: Tel Aviv.

This detailed and insightful memoir is chronologically structured. Its early part focuses on the author's turn toward Zionism as a youth and his connections with the democratic movement during and after World War I. He becomes a lawyer and works as legal counsel for a number of business associations during the Weimar years. The latter part of the memoir contains detailed descriptions of the expropriation of Jewish businesses by the Nazis. The author leaves Germany for Paris and Spain in 1933 and emigrates to Palestine in 1935.

111 pp., typescript, evaluation.

Lit.: Röder/Strauss.

253. "Anonymous", c/o Toni Angel, Haifa/Palestine; 31; Jewish; physician; last German residence: Vienna, 1940: Basel.

The manuscript consists of a detailed description of the author's concentration camp experiences at Dachau and Buchenwald. It contains hand-drawn maps of both camps.

56 pp., typescript, evaluation.

254. "Anonymous," c/o Alice Boehm, Cambridge/Massachusetts.

The file contains only some correspondence and an evaluation by the researchers. The manuscript was returned to the author in 1940.

255. [No author.]

This file contains only miscellaneous correspondence.

256. **Flambo, Hubertus** (pseudonym?); b: 1874; Protestant, m, ch: 3 (sons, daughter); physician; last German residence: Berlin, 1940: New York City.

This lengthy memoir describes the author's youth and student years, when he is active in a *Burschenschaft*. He becomes a physician and eventually leads the greater Berlin Medical Association until 1933. A conservative member of the medical establishment, he focuses on the medical community and its politicization during the Weimar Republic and the early Nazi years. He leaves directly for the U.S. in 1936.

228 pp., typescript, evaluation.

257. **Grünberg, Emile**; b: Vienna, economist, interpreter. Last German residence: Frankfurt, 1941: Chicago.

The author, son of the founder of the Institute for Social Research in Frankfurt, describes his youth and his student years in Frankfurt, where he observes the gradual shift toward corporate, right-wing thinking in all social classes. The changing climate among university students and teachers is the focus of his observations. A committed socialist and active in adult education in Frankfurt, the author leaves Germany in February 1933 to work as an interpreter for the International Labor Organization Geneva. From this vantage point he records the attempts of the Nazis to infiltrate Switzerland and the failed attempts of the new regime to gain respectability in the ILO.

87 pp. typescript, in English. Correspondence indicates that the manuscript was solicited by the Harvard organizers in 1941 and that the author received a $30.00 honorarium.

Lit.: GV, NUC.

258. Lenneberg, Robert; b: June 24, 1887, small town in Western Germany [Rheydt] d: [1965]; m, ch: 2 (sons), physician; last German residence: Düsseldorf, 1940: Rio de Janeiro.

The author is a professionally successful pediatrician whose liberal sympathies attract hostility from the SA before 1933. Unusually prescient, he and his wife begin considering emigration as early as 1932 despite the more sanguine view of those around them. The family leaves Germany for Rio de Janeiro in May 1933. Written in 1935 as part of a longer memoir, this factual and detailed account focuses on the years 1932-33.

285 pp., typescript, evaluation.

Lit.: Röder/Strauss (Eric Lenneberg).

259. Gerhard Müller; b: April 30, 1919, Halle/Saale; s; Jewish; last German residence: Halle, 1940: Wald-Schönengrund, Switzerland.

The son of a leather manufacturer, the author leaves the Gymnasium prematurely to work in various business internships. He emigrates to Geneva in spring 1937 and from there goes to Italy. With the help of relatives, he makes his way back to Switzerland, where he is placed in a mental hospital. The somewhat confused account intersperses the author's description of his psychological difficulties with political commentary.

140 pp., typescript.

260. Peech, Sibyl; b: Oct. 29, 1903 [d. Aug. 8, 1971, New York]. Dresden; Protestant, m; writer, film producer; last German residence: Berlin, 1940: Chicago.

From a patrician Dresden family, the author rebels against the authority of her parents and eventually finds her way to the film industry in Berlin, where she works in film production and later as a freelance author. Her account focuses on the years 1931-1935 and the transformation of German society as observed from within the film industry. Her direct and sometimes sarcastic style manifests her impatience with the passivity of the German public as Hitler takes power. Peech's account of speeches given by Carl von Ossietzky, Goebbels and of a conversation with the critic Alfred Kerr are particularly memorable. The author leaves Berlin in May 1935 for London and moves to Chicago in 1938.

181 pp., typescript, in English.

Lit.: Röder/Strauss (Moholy-Nagy, Sybil, née Pietzsch); GV (Moholy Nagy, Sybil); NUC (Moholy-Nagy, Dorothea Maria Pauline Alice Sybille).

261. Sabatzky, Kurt. b: [April 23, 1892], Köslin/Pommern [d. June 17, 1955, London]; m, ch:1 (daughter), lawyer, last German residence: Leipzig, 1940: London.

This journal-like chronicle begins in November 1918 with a description of the author's activities for the DDP. The account shows the life of a politically active lawyer who also becomes a high-ranking official of the Centralverein deutscher Staatsbürger jüdischen Glaubens. Sabatzky describes the struggle against the Nazis beginning in the 1920s from the viewpoint of a Centralverein leader and lawyer. He also describes how Jews could use courts and police to fight Nazi actions. Incarcerated in Buchenwald in 1938, he leaves for England in late August 1939, where he is interned for two months.

64 pp., typescript, two copies in file; correspondence indicates that the manuscript was solicited by the Harvard organizers and written in September 1941. It was not part of the essay contest.

Lit.: Röder/Strauss, GV, Limberg/Rübsaat. A selection from a later memoir by this author appears in Richarz, vol. 3.

262. Sevin, Barbara. (Mrs. W. Schütz), 27. b: [1912] near Berlin, m., Lutheran. Writer. Last German residence: Munich, 1941: London.

From a patrician family of academics and civil servants, the author attends university in Heidelberg and as an exchange student in Rhode Island. After returning to Heidelberg in 1939 she tries to maneuver uneasily between non-conformists and Nazis among her teachers and fellow students. A nuanced portrait of social and political shifts in different regions of Germany emerges from her descriptions of university life and *Arbeitsdienst* (labor service). Known for her outspokenness in the University of Heidelberg, she manages to finish her Ph.D. there but moves to Munich. Threatened with arrest, she moves to London in 1939.

357 pp., typescript.

Lit.: Röder/Strauss (Wilhelm Wolfgang Schütz).

263. "Anonymous"; b: 1898, Prague; Jewish, divorced; civil servant, writer; last German residence: Berlin (?).

Listed by this number, this manuscript is not a memoir, but consists of a socio-historical analysis of Central Europe from the late nineteenth to the mid-twentieth century. It contains no biographical information on the author.

147 pp., typescript, evaluation.

# INDEX

This index list only a selection of important topics for each entry, providing an initial orientation for scholars wishing to use the collection. Important place names, institutions, persons, and significant themes are indexed; frequently recurring items such as "antisemitism," "Hitler," "Nazis," and "middle class" have been omitted. Numbers refer to the file numbers of the "My Life in Germany" collection at Houghton Library and in the catalogue portion of this work.

* * * * * * * * * * * * * * * * * * * * * * * * * * * * * * *

www.ingramcontent.com/pod-product-compliance
Lightning Source LLC
Chambersburg PA
CBHW081139300726
48982CB00006B/1009

*9780871699138*